T0150748

The Beatles
on the Roof

The Beatles
on the Roof

Tony Barrell

OMNIBUS PRESS

London / New York / Paris / Sydney / Copenhagen / Berlin / Madrid / Tokyo

Copyright © 2017 Tony Barrell.
This edition copyright © 2017 Omnibus Press.
(A Division of Music Sales Limited)

Cover designed by Michael Bell Design.
Picture research by Kate Booker.

ISBN 978.1.78558.578.4
Order No. OP57343

The right of Tony Barrell to be identified as the author
of this Work has been asserted by him inaccordance with
the Copyright, Designs and Patents Act 1988.
All rights reserved. No part of this book may be reproduced
in any form or by any electronic ormechanical means,
including information storage or retrieval systems,
without permission in writing from the publisher,
except by a reviewer who may quote brief passages.

Exclusive Distributors:

Music Sales Limited
14/15 Berners Street
London W1T 3LJ
United Kingdom

Music Sales Pty. Limited
(Australia & New Zealand)
Level 4, 30–32 Carrington Street
Sydney NSW 2000
Australia

Every effort has been made to trace the copyright holders of
the photographs in this book but one or two were unreachable.
We would be grateful if the photographers concerned would contact us.

Printed in Malta.

A catalogue record for this book is available from the British Library.

www.omnibuspress.com

Contents

Preface

The Beatles' rooftop performance is often described as a "spontaneous" event: an iconic burst of rock'n'roll that came without warning out of a clear blue (or cloudy grey) sky. It's a nice story: that one random winter's day – January 30, 1969 – the greatest band in the land decided on the spur of the moment to entertain London with some songs they'd just thrown together, and grabbed their instruments and tramped up to the very top of their Mayfair headquarters, which just seemed the natural thing to do, plugged in and blasted away.

It *was* spontaneous insofar as it only became a definite plan moments before it happened. Indeed, it came very close to not happening at all. But the music that The Beatles played on that day was shaped by a panoply of occurrences and influences, both within the lives of the group and in the wider world. And the concert occurred as the culmination of a long sequence of ideas, conversations and conflicts. Expert technicians and loyal roadies worked like Trojans to make it happen. The Beatles themselves had sweated over those songs for weeks. And behind it all was a story of discord, discontent and discarded dreams, and a year of madness. If The Beatles made it all look easy, well, that was one of the things they were good at.

Most people call it the "rooftop concert", so that's what I usually call it. However, while it certainly took place on a rooftop, it wasn't really a concert. When you go to a concert, the musicians don't usually play a public sound check followed by a rehearsal of a song and then a proper version of it. But that's what The Beatles were doing: they were doing *takes* of their songs. That's what you do in a recording session, which is what it was. Except that it was more than that, as well.

It was an outdoor recording session for an album, and it was filmed, because it was intended as the finale to a television show. So it was like a reality-TV version of a recording session, but transplanted from a comfortable studio to a lofty urban location in the depths of winter. Insanity!

In a way, it was just The Beatles being The Beatles, pushing the boundaries and making news again. Although they were still in their twenties (John Lennon and Ringo Starr were 28, Paul McCartney was 26 and George Harrison was 25), they had a lifetime of achievements to look back on. They had sold records by the lorryload, pioneered stadium pop concerts in America, been awarded MBEs, recorded a concept album, taken LSD, recorded instruments backwards, performed on the first ever global satellite TV show, started their own record label and swanned off to India to discover the meaning of life. Although they weren't the first rock band to play on top of a building, the rooftop event was another of those achievements – something else to put in the history books and give them a medal for.

It was also a "happening", the kind of arty-but-really-a-bit-silly event that was terribly hip in the sixties. Happenings took many different forms: hippies might dress up as nuns and roll around in maple syrup, or 100 metaphysical poets might walk from John O'Groats to Land's End while repeating the word "trousers" over and over again, and people would watch and feel somehow enriched by the experience. It was conceptual art. This particular happening was all about The Beatles appearing in public when many people thought they had split up, playing entirely new songs while withstanding the freezing cold, annoying the neighbours and resisting arrest by the boys in blue.

The rooftop event can be seen as a few other things as well. It was a bonding exercise for the group, a means of reminding each other why they came together in the first place. It was a mystic ritual to renew the spirit of the band after a period of personal disharmony and misfortune. And it was an anti-establishment prank, a wheeze to get the goat of their snooty Mayfair neighbours, especially the tut-tutting Savile Row tailors with their conservative tendencies.

It was also a kind of self-audition. They hadn't played live in public for about two-and-a-half years and were beginning to wonder if they could still do it, so here was the big test. In that respect, they showed enormous courage. If they'd failed, they knew the media would have been circling like vultures, dashing off nasty reviews and hatchet jobs with relish: The Beatles are finished; they've lost their magic; did they ever have any magic in the first place, really? Have we all been conned? Were they really the Emperor's New Clothes? It would have been like *Magical Mystery Tour* all over again, but worse. Fortunately, of course, they passed the self-audition.

And yet, despite its multifaceted nature, the rooftop performance is so often regarded in shallow, simplistic terms. On big anniversaries, when the year ends in a '9', it gets an article here and there and maybe a short piece on TV, most of them rehashing the same list of facts: it was on a roof, Ringo Starr wore his wife's coat, people stopped and stared, the police came and shut it down, John Lennon made a joke at the end. The reasons why it happened, and why it happened in the way it did, go largely unexplored.

Looking back on The Beatles' career history, it becomes evident that the main story of the rooftop concert begins with the launch of their own company, Apple, in 1968. Most obviously, Apple gave them the actual roof on which they would ultimately perform, because this entire building was the company's new Mayfair headquarters. Moreover, the year 1968 saw both John Lennon and Paul McCartney establish new and lasting romantic relationships, which they would sing about on that roof. This was also the year in which the band embarked on their *Get Back* project, originally foreseen as a TV special for The Beatles (it later morphed into the *Let It Be* film and album), and the high point and culmination of that project was the rooftop session.

It seems artificial and unsatisfying to tell this story as if it occurred in a vacuum. It very much belongs to the closing years of the sixties, when the naive, blissed-out dreams of flower-power summers had already lost their lustre. This was a time when young people were marching for a whole range of causes: standing up for civil rights, women's rights and nuclear disarmament, and opposing the Vietnam War and other policies of old-fashioned, draconian governments. The Beatles, especially John Lennon, were committed to many of those causes, and Apple itself was a kind of pressure group as well as a business enterprise, seeking to find a new, more inclusive and creative form of capitalism for the world to follow.

Meanwhile, as the youth of the day were striving to invent a better global future, the British police were routinely busting famous musicians for possession of trifling quantities of drugs, and inviting their friends from the gutter press to come and enjoy the fun. In 1968, everybody had a hard year.

The rooftop concert, as an early piece of reality TV, emerged from a period when musicians were finding new ways to engage with the media of film and television. Elvis Presley used TV to stage a remarkable "live" comeback, while The Rolling Stones and

Jefferson Airplane were toying with *cinéma vérité* and collaborating with the radical *Nouvelle Vague* director Jean-Luc Godard.

Understanding the rooftop concert also requires an appreciation of The Beatles' late-sixties musical stance, the end result of the strange destiny they had created for themselves. Their story is one of a band that continually escaped from an undesirable situation, only to find themselves caught in a trap from which they needed to escape again. Initially they escaped working-class conventionality and anonymity to become the darlings of Britain and the world; but that brought the relentless grind of Beatlemania, wherein they lost much of their privacy and travelled the globe playing music that was drowned out by the screams of young women for whom the music was secondary to the band's physical appeal. The Beatles escaped from Beatlemania via the radical decision of calling a halt to playing live altogether, and retreated into the studio to make elaborately textured, beautifully handcrafted music that they had no intention of performing live.

By 1969 they had decided that *that* was a trap as well. Now, disenchanted with the technical complexity of their recent music, they wanted to get back to basics, play like a straightforward rock'n'roll outfit again, in the spirit of rootsy American groups like The Band. But when The Beatles reconvened in January 1969 for the *Get Back* project, their old Fab Four camaraderie disintegrating horribly, they discovered that just playing rock'n'roll together was yet another trap. Eventually, their escape from that one would be the dissolution of the group.

This is what makes the *Let It Be* film a tough watch. The Beatles, who once appeared capable of bottling happiness with their music, were now bottling misery. But the shining moment in that movie, like the pearl produced by the grit in the oyster, is the rooftop performance.

For my book I've spoken to several people who were around The Beatles in 1968, and several more who were present on that chilly January day in Savile Row, some of them working with the group but many of them passers-by who were there through good fortune and happy coincidence. I've taken to calling these witnesses "Savile Row celebrities", partly because they seem to like it, and because I think they are, or should be, celebrities of a kind. Because this was 1969, most of these people are of a reasonably advanced age now, but I've been pleasantly surprised by the sharpness of their memories.

This story does have a personal dimension for me. I was a small boy in short trousers when I heard that The Beatles had played an unannounced concert in London, and I was inconsolable. Why couldn't they have given me, one of their biggest fans, some warning that they were doing it? It would surely have been worth skipping primary school to go to London for. Ever since then, I've wished I had been there that day, and I've developed a fascination for the event that won't go away.

I wrote the first draft of this preface while standing on a cold and sunny day in Savile Row, across the road from the smart Georgian brick building where The Beatles surprised the world all those years ago. If you're ever in this sacred street on one of the anniversaries of January 30, 1969, perhaps we'll get to meet. It's where I go every year to capture the "vibes" of the rooftop performance that I missed all those years ago. If you cock an ear in a certain direction and use your imagination, they're still there to be heard and enjoyed.

Tony Barrell, Savile Row, 2017

Acknowledgements

During my research I was lucky enough to speak to Deborah Scarfe (née Wellum), who was the receptionist at Apple Corps from 1968. She gave me a wonderful interview, with her memory of so many events apparently undimmed by time. I was very sad to hear that Deborah passed away recently. This book is dedicated to her.

I'm very grateful to the many other people I interviewed who were in London back in January 1969. I have put the memories of these witnesses to the test, and they all passed the audition. Special thanks are due to Michael Lindsay-Hogg, Peter Brown, Vicki Wickham, Paul Bond, Barbara O'Donnell, Dave Harries, Kevin Harrington, Ray Shayler, Ken Wharfe, Chris O'Dell, Steve Lovering, David Martin, Andy Taylor, Leslie Healy, Paula Marshall, Vince Lankin, Sidney Ruback, Malcolm Plewes, Alan Bennett and Keith Altham.

I'm also grateful to my editor, Chris Charlesworth, and to everybody who helped with the research, notably the former Bow Street Policeman Dave Allen, the staff of the British Library, and various other experts; to the devoted Beatles fan Caroline Lennon for some inspiring conversations on rooftop anniversaries in Savile Row; and to Carrie Kania and Robin Morgan for all their help, encouragement and enthusiasm.

CHAPTER ONE

Everybody Had A Hard Year

When John Lennon sang from the rooftop that "Everybody had a hard year", the sentiment resonated with a lot of people. The year 1968 was fresh in the memory as a period of upheaval and unrest, of strikes, protests, violence and youth rebellion. This was the year when the Vietnam War intensified, students and workers fought with police in the barricaded streets of Paris, Martin Luther King and Bobby Kennedy were assassinated, Russian tanks rolled into Czechoslovakia, and the USA elected one of its worst-ever presidents.

Nevertheless it was a good year for experimental cinema, controversial theatre, alternative religion and audacious space travel. It was also the year when both John Lennon and Paul McCartney began their most intense romantic relationships, which they would celebrate in song on the most famous roof in pop music.

But life had also been tough in Beatle Land. At the start of 1968 they had to recover from the critical mauling given to their fantasy coach-ride extravaganza *Magical Mystery Tour*, shown to a bemused audience of Christmas TV viewers, and did so with a kind of cleansing ritual that saw them studying Transcendental Meditation

1

at the feet of an Indian guru, and by attempting to redefine the rules of business with a benevolent new company, Apple Corps, that all but promised to turn the whole world into Beatles. After a prodigious gush of songwriting in India, they threw themselves into recording with such vigour that they finished up with a double album.

While they gave it the unifying title of *The Beatles*, they became more fragmented than ever before while making it, with individual members often tinkering with their own songs in different studios. It seemed that the logical thing to do after the White Album, as it became known, would have been to separate there and then, and begin four exciting solo careers. But no, now they had their own business to run, and they were obliged to pull together and make it work — at least for a while.

John suddenly fell so hard for the artist Yoko Ono that he not only had to leave his cosy family life with Cynthia and little Julian, but he also became almost subsumed by his new relationship, for which he had to withstand mockery from critics and members of the public who had never seen a Japanese conceptual artist before, and a degree of scepticism from the other Beatles. Consolation came after Paul converted the sorrow of John's estranged wife and five-year-old child into one of his most infectious songs, altering 'Hey Jules' to 'Hey Jude' along the way, and it became the biggest-selling single The Beatles would release. And the early days of Apple, at least, were happy ones.

Apple had begun as an accountant's wheeze to reduce the group's tax burden by giving them something to do with their wealth, but it quickly blossomed into one of the most generous, idealistic enterprises ever seen. The company wanted to give aspiring musicians and songwriters a leg-up and a helping hand, rewarding talent with recording contracts and a crack at the big time.

On its simplest level, Apple was a talent-scouting enterprise – a cooler version of the contemporary television show *Opportunity Knocks*, which turned the spotlight on unknown singers, musclemen and performing dogs. In March 1968 the music paper *Disc & Music Echo* teamed up with the company to launch a nationwide hunt for the next pop sensation, announcing: "Apple, the company set up by The Beatles to discover, sign and promote new pop talent, are rightly aware that all over Britain there are hundreds of unheard-of groups who, with the right handling, could be every bit as big as today's top pop names."

Disc was asking readers to find the talent themselves, and to vote for the top beat combo in their local area. Apple would then count all the votes, send talent scouts across the country to see the readers' most favoured bands, and then finally name "the group they have signed to a recording contract and the full promotional facilities of the Apple organisation". Six "lucky readers" who voted for the winning group would then win prizes, including a voucher for £25 to spend on far-out clothes from the Apple Boutique in Baker Street.

On April 20, Apple splashed out on advertisements in British newspapers, showing a photograph of company staffer Alistair Taylor as a one-man band, strumming a guitar and with a bass drum on his back, beneath the headline "This man has talent…". The advert asked for people to record themselves singing their songs and send a tape to Apple's Baker Street address. This is what the singer in the picture had done, it playfully pretended, and now he was rich. "This man now owns a Bentley!" it claimed.

On its most profound level, Apple was a bold attempt to bring the radicalism and experimentalism of modern music, art, cinema and theatre into the stuffy world of business. John and Paul, in particular, saw it as no less than a utopian new model for enterprise, in which unfettered creativity took precedence over profit. It wouldn't be just a record company: it would make films, electronic gadgets, clothing, furniture, books and whatever else it wanted to; there was even talk of it having its own schools for children. Not long after it expanded into premises in Wigmore Street in the West End of London that year, the Apple concept had grown so rapidly that it was looking for a larger headquarters.

On the same day that the Apple press advert appeared, a British politician struck a very different tone, sending out a message of intolerance and fear that appeared to legitimise xenophobia in the United Kingdom. The 55-year-old Conservative politician Enoch Powell, then shadow defence secretary, gave a long speech in which he criticised proposed race-relations legislation and warned about the long-term effects of immigration in Britain. He was troubled by the influx of Asian men and women from Kenya who had failed to acquire citizenship status from the former British colony after its independence. Thousands of them had been denied work permits as the Kenyan government pursued a policy of Africanisation, but they were entitled to British passports.

Speaking to a roomful of fellow Conservatives in Birmingham, Powell warned: "In 15 or 20 years, on present trends, there will be in this country three-and-a-half million Commonwealth immigrants and their descendants." His own forecast for the year 2000 was that the Commonwealth immigrants would number "in the region of five to seven million, approximately one-tenth of the whole population, and approaching that of Greater London. Of course, it will not be evenly distributed from Margate to Aberystwyth and from Penzance to Aberdeen. Whole areas, towns and parts of towns across England will be occupied by sections of the immigrant and immigrant-descended population."

The line in Powell's monologue that appeared to lend it gravitas (and would give it its popular title, the "Rivers of Blood speech") was: "As I look ahead, I am filled with foreboding; like the Roman, I seem to see 'the River Tiber foaming with much blood'."

The day after the rant, Powell was sacked from the Shadow Cabinet by the Conservative leader, Edward Heath. Powell was widely criticised for his inflammatory words, which inspired demonstrations by white Britons chanting for the repatriation (and worse) of non-white immigrants – as he must have expected. Porters from Smithfield meat market marched to the Houses of Parliament in their bloodstained overalls, chanting jingoistic songs and carrying placards demanding that Powell be awarded a George Cross. What Powell surely never imagined is that the national conversation he triggered, as we shall see, would inspire the lyrics of The Beatles.

In May, John and Paul flew to New York to publicise the launch of Apple. They were accompanied by Alexis Mardas, the young Greek inventor dubbed "Magic Alex" who had charmed them with his futuristic ideas and gadgets, and who would head up the electronics division of the new company.

The idea was that creative people could approach Apple and have their brilliant ideas turned into reality, without all the usual hang-ups of everyday capitalism that the band themselves had endured when they signed to EMI. "We want to help people," explained Paul, "but without doing it like a charity. We always had to go to the big men on our knees and touch our forelocks and say, 'Please can we do so-and-so?' We're in the happy position of not needing any more money, so for the first time the bosses aren't in it for the profit. If you come to me and say, 'I've had such-and-such a dream,' I'll say to you, 'Go away and do it.'" Daringly, at a New York press conference on May 14, 1968 – in the middle of the Cold War, with Vietnam still a bloody battleground and the Sorbonne in Paris occupied by anti-establishment students – Paul likened the new business to "a kind of Western communism". Less than 20 years earlier America had been in the grip of McCarthyism, in which many Americans prominent in the world of entertainment and literature were arrested on charges, often spurious, of being communists.

"The Beatles at a certain point wanted to be good for the world," says Michael Lindsay-Hogg, the American director who would conceive and film the rooftop concert. "They'd been told they were good for the world and they wanted to actually *be* good for the world, if they could. They wanted to offer people the means to realise their dreams and their ambitions, given that they were consistent with what The Beatles thought were good dreams or good ambitions."

At a time when moral guardians such as Mary Whitehouse were campaigning vigorously against "filth" in the arts, Apple was also a libertarian enterprise with its own permissive moral code, unsaddled with unhip notions of obscenity. So when both George and John took a liking to the song 'The King of Fuh', by an American singer calling himself Brute Force, which repeatedly and outrageously sang the praises of "the Fuh King", it seemed a perfect choice for the new label.

Apple was now a powerful magnet for all kinds of artists, musicians, fantasists and fruitcakes who needed money to realise their creative dreams. The Beatles' publicist Derek Taylor summed up the madness of it all in his distinctive, entertaining way: "A time-and-motion man would have lost his reason in those days in Wigmore Street. I had a slim shoebox of a room and such were our promises of a hearing for anyone with something creative to offer; anyone off the street who was frustrated with years of screaming for someone to listen; any singer who could climb a scale; anyone with a piece of coloured paper which he called a painting; any caller with rhyme he believed to be poetry; any Fellini of the 1970s. Such was our published pledge to be a market place for the lowly artist, a gathering of Beautiful People, that by dusk any night there could be a duo of guitarists 'better than Clapton', a Mancunian who saw himself as a mingling of 'Mr. Kite', 'John Wesley Harding', 'Billy Shears', 'The Mighty Quinn' and 'Popeye the Sailor Man' and having thus seen, sought £50,000 to make a film of him acting out the fantasy, California author-to-be with hair like a hedge in Heswell, a sculptress who had never sculpted but who wanted facilities to make a nude out of patent leather and then cover it in oil to induce 'tactile delight'..."

As more songwriters' tapes and artists' proposals flooded into Apple, the company was drawing up grandiose ideas for a bigger headquarters that could accommodate their expanding ambitions. "The original idea was to buy a whole estate, so we could all go and live on it," Alistair Taylor recalled later. "There'd be a big dome in the middle, which would be Apple, and then there'd be four corridors leading to four large houses, one for John, one for Paul, one for George and one for Ringo. And around the estate, there would be some other houses, sort of gardeners' domes, and we'd live in there. One way or another a good time would be had by all. Well, the reality was that they did try and buy an estate, but, with land being what it is, the nearest place we could get was Norwich, and nobody could see us running a record company out of Norwich, crazy though we were."

While his wife Cynthia was holidaying in Greece in May 1968, John Lennon invited Yoko Ono to his home in Kenwood, Surrey, where the Beatle and the artist made some avant-garde recordings and then made love for the first time. Cynthia returned home late one afternoon, venturing into the morning room: "When I opened the door a scene that took my breath and voice away confronted me. Dirty breakfast dishes were cluttering the table, the curtains were closed and the room was dimly lit. Facing me was John, sitting relaxed in his dressing gown. With her back to me and equally relaxed and at home, was Yoko. The only response I received was 'Oh, hi,' from both parties. They looked so right together."

John later remembered how he had fallen for Yoko, and how she had even become like a drug for him: "I had never known love like this before, and it hit me so hard that I had to halt my marriage to Cynthia. My marriage to Cynthia was not unhappy, but it was just a normal marital state where nothing happened and which we continued to sustain. You sustain it until you meet someone who suddenly sets you alight. With Yoko I really knew love for the first time. Our attraction for each other was a mental one… I just realised that she knew everything I knew and more, probably, and that it was coming out of a woman's head. It just bowled me over. It was like finding gold or something. As she was talking to me, I would get high, and the discussions would get to such a level that I would be going higher and higher."

John and Yoko were first seen out in public on May 22, though the event was missed by the paparazzi, who were not yet clued in about the Beatle's extramarital relationship. Yoko tagged along when John and George attended the opening of a second Apple clothing shop. This was Apple Tailoring (Civil and Theatrical) at 161 New King's Road, run by the Australian designer John Crittle, and a more sober establishment than the Apple Boutique. "The Beatles' dress sense is quietening down now, like everyone else," said Crittle. "They all went mad last year, but now they're all coming back to a normal way of life. We won't get teenyboppers here, because prices will be too high for them. We're pushing velvet jackets and the Regency look, although The Beatles put forward plenty of suggestions. They have pretty far-ahead ideas, actually. We're catering mainly for pop groups, personalities and turned-on swingers."

John Lennon wasn't really dressed for the part of a celebrity cutting the ribbon on a tailoring business that day. He wore a thick brown fur coat that he was clearly fond of, because he is seen wearing it in many photographs from that period. He's sporting the same coat in a photograph taken with a few fans outside Paul's house in Cavendish Avenue, and in some of the shots taken in July during The Beatles' Mad Day Out – a tour of London for publicity purposes, in which the band was accompanied by a series of photographers. And he's wearing it again in photographs taken with Eric Clapton and members of The Who and The Rolling Stones in December 1968. This would also be the coat that kept him reasonably warm for the duration of the rooftop concert. Commentators often trot out the line that this was Yoko's coat and he borrowed it for the performance, but there is plenty of photographic evidence to suggest otherwise.

John and Yoko's first official appearance together came on June 15, when they contributed a joint work of art to the National Sculpture Exhibition at Coventry Cathedral. The piece consisted of a circular white garden bench over two white flowerpots, placed on a symbolic east-west axis, in which two acorns were to be planted to celebrate their love and promote world peace. However, church authorities decreed that because John and Yoko weren't married the acorns should not be planted on consecrated ground, so they were planted in ordinary ground nearby instead.

They were becoming pacifist artists and campaigners at a time when the world seemed an especially violent place. On April 4, the civil-rights leader Martin Luther King had been shot dead in Memphis, Tennessee, where he had been working on plans for a Poor People's March on Washington, DC. On June 10, the presidential hopeful Senator Robert Kennedy was assassinated in Los Angeles. Two days before that, the artist Andy Warhol had been shot and injured by the radical feminist Valerie Solanis at his

Manhattan studio, The Factory. The Vietnam War was still raging, and the American death toll alone would exceed 14,000 by the end of the year.

By the summer of 1968 The Beatles had begun recording the White Album. On June 20, John used all three studios at EMI in Abbey Road to begin assembling his experimental sound collage 'Revolution 9', while Paul McCartney flew to Los Angeles, where he would address a sales conference held by Capitol Records, The Beatles' American label. Not far away from that record-company bash, Elvis Presley was embarking on a series of performances in Hollywood that would become part of his 'Comeback Special', to be broadcast on American television towards the end of the year. One night after Elvis had been rehearsing, the show's director, Steve Binder, found the singer chatting with other musicians and jamming in his dressing room, playing old blues and rock'n'roll numbers for the sheer fun of it. Binder was excited to see music being made in such a relaxed setting, and was inspired to include a similar informal jam session in the TV special, which was recorded at NBC's Burbank Studios.

After their hectic and debilitating tours of 1966, The Beatles had called a halt to live performances. This wasn't surprising: they'd received death threats for playing the Budokan martial-arts venue in Japan, were roughed up after causing a major diplomatic incident in the Philippines and were in fear of their lives in America's Bible Belt after religious zealots took John's fairly innocent remarks about Christianity out of context. They had cleverly fortified the decision not to tour again by immersing themselves in the studio, where they had much more time to create elaborate multi-track recordings that would have been impossible for the four of them to replicate live even if people wanted them to.

But the group's refusal to play any live concerts was leaving a vacuum that was being filled by all kinds of speculation about the group returning to the stage. The latest edition of *Melody Maker* had a front-page story claiming there was an "exciting prospect" that they would soon play Moscow. It was all based on the flimsy story that the impresario Vic Lewis was negotiating with the Soviet authorities with the aim of putting on Russian gigs by a variety of Western acts, which included Donovan, Nina Simone and Andy Williams. Lewis, who had worked with Brian Epstein and was now running the late Beatles manager's NEMS Enterprises, said: "I'd also like to set up a trip by The Beatles. I haven't said anything to them yet, but it could be the sort of offer the boys would be keen to accept. I feel they might regard it as something of a challenge."

Lewis added that he didn't believe they would tour Britain again. "They can't be expected to play the type of music they have put on records like *Sgt. Pepper* – with their use of electronic effects – on stage." Puzzlingly, he didn't explain why that wouldn't be a problem in the Russian capital.

Turning its attention from the East Anglian backwaters of Norwich to London, Apple found a gem of a building that was up for sale in the prestigious Mayfair district, and paid £500,000 for it. Years later, Paul McCartney remembered Neil Aspinall, The Beatles' former road manager and then manager of Apple Corps, making the discovery: "I had asked Neil to look for a great London building. And he found it, 3 Savile Row – Lady Hamilton's London residence, which Nelson bought for her. I thought, if nothing else, that's a good London building."

It was a certainly a handsome thing – a five-storey Georgian brick mansion with plenty of room to accommodate the dreams and schemes of The Beatles' exciting new enterprise. And the tale that Admiral Nelson, hero of the Napoleonic Wars, had purchased the building as a residence for his famous lover, Emma, Lady

Hamilton, came as a bonus. The mention of Hamilton may have held extra fascination because she had been born in humble circumstances in a place The Beatles knew well: the Wirral, in Merseyside.

The alleged Hamilton connection with the Apple building has since been cited many times since 1968. However, it doesn't stand up to research. For one thing, the home that Nelson and Lady Hamilton shared in Merton, Surrey, has often been described as the only house that Nelson ever owned. For another, historians have dismissed his connection with No. 3 Savile Row. Asked about the story, Kate Williams, author of *England's Mistress: The Infamous Life Of Emma Hamilton*, replied: "I'm afraid it's not true," adding that many British buildings carry the suspect cachet of having been bought by Nelson for his mistress.

Flora Fraser, author of *Beloved Emma: The Life Of Emma, Lady Hamilton*, is also sceptical: "This house was owned by William Wellesley-Pole, sometime Master of the Mint during the time Nelson and Emma were romantically involved, prior to the admiral's death in 1805. Wellesley-Pole did not live in the house but rented it out. It is possible that Nelson leased it for a short time for Emma during the months following her husband, Sir William's death in 1803 and prior to his own death at Trafalgar. But I am not sure when."

So the house was never bought for Lady Hamilton. There remains the possibility that it was leased or rented for her, but it's extremely unlikely. After it was built around 1753, it appears to have been continuously occupied by other people; there isn't any room in the building's history for her to fit in, even as a humble tenant. She and Nelson are known to have lived – separately – in a series of other Mayfair locations, but not here. The Hamilton story about No. 3 may well have been invented one day by somebody involved in the sale of the property, and there is a likely candidate.

Basil Dighton bought the house in 1913. He was an apparently respectable antiques dealer, and one of his clients was a businessman called Adolph Shrager. By 1923, Shrager had paid Dighton £84,887 (about $400,000) for some antique furniture, which Dighton claimed had come from Royston Hall. But Schrager soon discovered he'd been sold fakes. The case went to court, where an antiques expert was highly critical of the furniture. There was no such place as Royston Hall, and of the Chippendale lamp stands Shrager had bought, the expert said: "The legs were obviously new, and the stem had probably been made from a child's four-post bed. The price of £450 was ridiculous. As second-hand furniture they would be worth £8/10s." A Queen Anne cabinet, costing £850, "was not Queen Anne, but was recently made up in a factory". Bizarrely, Shrager didn't win the case, because it was deemed that the recently manufactured pieces included some old elements, so Dighton was justified in selling them as antiques. But if he was prepared to lie about "Royston Hall" and a stack of fake antiques, he might have initiated the fib about Hamilton living here.

By the thirties, 3 Savile Row had become a gentlemen's club, the Albany, which hosted snooker tournaments, served gourmet food and attracted many of the famous faces of the day. The club thrived into the fifties, when a travel guide claimed: "Anybody from Tyrone Power to Gracie Fields to Bob Hope might be at the next table." In 1955 the Albany Club was purchased by Jack Hylton, who had enjoyed a successful career as a bandleader but was now a big-time impresario, with a huge roster of singers and comedians, and production credits on many London theatre shows. Shortly after buying it, he turned the place into his spacious offices, Hylton House, and started presenting television variety shows from the building – though not from the rooftop, sadly.

Jack Hylton died in January 1965, and three years later his estate sold the building to The Beatles.

Regardless of the house's history, the name "Savile Row" would have appealed to The Beatles on a subconscious level. Not only did it have the same rhythm as the name of their beloved recording studio, Abbey Road, and a similar sound, but it would also have reminded them of the Saville Theatre, which Brian Epstein had leased from 1965 for rock shows as well as stage plays. Chuck Berry, Jimi Hendrix, The Who and Cream had all played the Saville, and The Beatles had used it to make their promo film for the single 'Hello, Goodbye'.

And they were more familiar with the district of Mayfair than many people imagined. For several weeks in late 1963 they had actually lived here, sharing a three-bedroom apartment on the fifth storey of 57 Green Street. Brian Epstein had taken them to the hairdresser Leonard of Mayfair, in Upper Grosvenor Street, as part of his plan to smarten up the group's image. They had recorded sessions for radio shows in Aeolian Hall in New Bond Street, and socialised with Smokey Robinson in 1964 at the White Elephant club in Curzon Street – where Epstein liked to indulge his gambling habit. They had also come to Curzon Street in July 1963 to pose for photographs at the Washington Hotel, including a prophetic shot of the quartet standing on the roof of the building, among the chimney pots, with Mayfair spread out beneath them.

After paying half a million pounds for No. 3 Savile Row, Apple set about redecorating the building to create a headquarters worthy of Britain's hippest new organisation. Gallons of white paint were used to brighten the gloomy walls and woodwork, as well as the front door and the metal railings outside. This immediately made the premises stand out from the others in the neighbourhood, which followed the tradition of having jet-black railings and sober-coloured doors. Huge rolls of apple-green carpet were brought in to soften the floors. Trendy tables, chairs and chandeliers were custom-made for the offices, with specifications to suit the predilections of the Apple bigwigs.

The Beatles' business manager, Peter Brown, disliked smoking, but would often find himself in meetings with the band in which they all lit up. To mitigate the problem, he had a special item of furniture made for his vast office on the building's second storey. "A friend of mine introduced me to this furniture designer, and I commissioned him to make me a desk," he says. "On the other side of the desk was a shelf below the top, where I put the ashtrays – so they'd have to put their cigarettes on the ashtrays, below my eyeline. I don't know what ever happened to that desk. My room was also called the boardroom, because at one end there was an enormous octagonal table, which we also had specially made. When we had formal meetings, The Beatles and Neil and me, we did it at that table."

Nobody thought to do much with the flat roof, though the possibility of a lovely, lush roof garden was discussed. Even in their wildest LSD trips, The Beatles are unlikely to have imagined that in the depths of the following winter, this would be the site of one of their most legendary concerts.

Perhaps it is its long tradition of specialist, fine craftsmanship that sets Savile Row apart, and maybe there is a brittleness and vulnerability born of the street's location at the eastern edge of Mayfair and dangerously close to the less exalted, scuzzier area of Soho. There's no doubt that it is one of the most cliquey and conservative streets in Britain. Its name calls to mind a rarefied domain of twill, worsted and Prince of Wales checks – just as the name Harley Street evokes an exclusive world of top-flight private medicine and therapies. Novice cloth-cutters in "the Row" spend years learning the esoteric, centuries-old techniques of suit-making, and the clientele tends to be exclusive, because not every man about town can afford to splash several thousands of pounds on exquisite handcrafted clothing. Royals, aristocrats, senior politicians, high-ranking military men and movie stars all came here to be dressed.

According to The Beatles' late press officer Derek Taylor, there was some perceptible snootiness from the tailors after The Beatles moved into their exclusive domain. He later wrote: "The Apple business is in Savile Row, a street which believes itself to be awfully important. It lies behind Regent Street, another street which has a high opinion of itself. Both are in the Western End of London, glamourised sometime between the wars by the title 'West End', a phrase much affected by the media to suggest a beautiful way of life in which big band leaders and rich society people wined and dined and opined on the really essential things like oysters and champagne and staying up late and keeping things much the way they are, only better and bigger and finer.

"Savile Row didn't really welcome The Beatles. Many of the shopkeepers there, silly snobbish growly, obsequious people, believed that since they had been selling marvellous suits to marvellous people they had a right to be the *only* ones there, which is about as daft as you can get, for, as Lewis Carroll said, a cat *may* look at a king, though few enough choose to."

Despite what many people think, The Beatles weren't the first interlopers in Savile Row from the vulgar world of sixties pop music. Further down on the same side of the street, past many of the old bespoke establishments, was Aberbach House, a hotbed of songwriting and music publishing, at No. 17 – the house where the playwright Richard Sheridan had died. The British songsmith David Martin remembers working there in the sixties: "I was in a songwriting partnership with two other writers, Geoff Morrow and Chris Arnold, at Carlin Music, which was a music-publishing company owned by a lovely American guy called Freddy

Bienstock. The building in Savile Row was like a songwriters' workshop. There were lots of songwriters in the building: there was Clive Westlake, who wrote 'I Close My Eyes And Count To Ten' for Dusty Springfield; there were a couple of guys called Guy Fletcher and Doug Flett, who wrote hits for The Hollies and Cliff Richard; and then Geoff, Chris and I were in the basement. We had a company with The Shadows called Shadamm Music [the "Shad" representing the band and the "amm" for Arnold, Martin, Morrow], and we were all writing. The office for Cliff Richard and The Shadows was in that building as well, and they used to rehearse there."

It was at No. 17 that Bienstock presided over a myriad of companies representing the lucrative song catalogues of acts such as Elvis Presley, The Animals and various artists on Motown Records. Born in Switzerland, Bienstock had begun his career in the stockroom of the Brill Building, the famous songwriting hub in New York. Later he became a song plugger, before specialising in finding songs for Presley to sing in his movies.

"After Apple moved in to No 3. Savile Row," said David Martin, "there were The Beatles at one end of the street, and we were further down at No. 17, with all these wonderful tailors in between. We were like bookends. And I often wondered what all these tailors, with all their posh customers, thought about us ragamuffins from the music business coming into Savile Row. If you were a long-established, top-rate tailor making suits for the upper echelons and royalty and Christ knows what else, it must have been strange to see a whole bunch of music people: it was incongruous."

Early October 1966 was a noisy period for the Row, for this is where the Jimi Hendrix Experience was formed and played together for the first time. The guitarist came to No. 17 to rehearse with the bassist Noel Redding and to audition drummers for his

17

new band. After various candidates were tried out, they settled on Mitch Mitchell. And the cacophony they created here wasn't just loud electric music. Hendrix's manager, Chas Chandler, who had booked the rehearsal space, had given the band 30-watt Burns amplifiers, which they hated, and Hendrix and Mitchell tried to wreck them so that Chandler would have to replace them with better gear. The guitarist and the drummer went as far as throwing the amps down the stairs, though even this failed to destroy the resilient equipment.

In July 1968, before The Beatles installed themselves in their new domain, John Lennon had his own art exhibition, *You Are Here*, at the Robert Fraser Gallery in Duke Street, and on the opening day he released 365 helium-filled white balloons into the sky. Each one had a tag attached, asking the finder to write to John at the gallery's address. The result was an eye-opener: many people, the sixties equivalent of today's internet trolls, responded with abusive messages that took swipes at John and Yoko's relationship and called her a home-wrecker. All this came on top of snide comments in the media that mocked the couple and questioned the merit of Yoko's outlandish works of art.

Michael Lindsay-Hogg believes the 35-year-old conceptual artist was widely misunderstood in Britain at the time. "Yoko was a very important person in the artistic community of New York in the late fifties and early sixties, and when there were happenings and artists' soirées she would be in the centre of that world. But when she turned up in England nobody really knew, at least in the rock'n'roll world, who she was; nobody knew that she was someone of definite credentials. And in some ways, people did not treat her with the respect that she had earned already."

Apple, meanwhile, was treating too many creative people with too much respect. The business continued to fork out prodigious sums for a wide range of supposedly innovative projects, but was receiving poor returns on its investments. Ringo Starr later described some of the problems: "We'd give one guy 16mm movie equipment and another guy a tent to do a Punch and Judy show on a beach. They'd take the money and say, 'Well, maybe next week.' The artists who made records didn't let us down, but all the others did."

The young receptionist at Apple was Debbie Wellum, who remembers having to deal with some peculiar visitors looking for funding from the company – as when the building temporarily became a showcase for some "gonks": small fluffy toys with quirky faces. "These people came in; they were Europeans, I can't remember what country they were from, and they were completely off their heads and they came in and stuck gonks all over my wall in reception, and refused to leave until they saw a Beatle. And just at that point, John and Yoko came in. Their office was off reception, and they had a double mirror put in there so they could see who was in reception, though it didn't really work very well. John spoke to them and said he thought they should take their gonks off his wall. In the end, they took them down and were escorted out of the building."

Just two weeks after The Beatles moved into their plush new HQ, they had to admit defeat with their Apple Boutique in Baker Street, which was haemmorhaging money. After helping themselves to a few choice items, they gave away the rest of the stock to all comers – each customer being limited to one item – before closing its doors. Apple Tailoring also closed shortly afterwards. Paul explained that clothing retail just wasn't the right business for them: "Apple is mainly concerned with fun, not frocks. We want to devote our energies to records, films and our electronics adventures."

The fact that Paul had mentioned "films" increased speculation that, four years after *Help!*, The Beatles might be thinking about appearing in another full-length movie. The film-maker Jean-Luc Godard visited Apple one day for a meeting with Denis O'Dell, head of Apple Films, who suggested the Frenchman direct a documentary about the everyday lives of The Beatles. Godard agreed to do some conceptual development, and an outline contract was even drawn up with the Paramount film company. Denis suggested a title, which was meaningless but nonetheless appealed to him: *One Plus One*. But George Harrison, the most private and pragmatic Beatle, disliked the idea of making the film, so the project was scrapped.

On Thursday, August 22, as The Beatles devoted their energies to the song 'Back In The USSR' for the White Album at Abbey Road, the atmosphere in the studio thickened in the vicinity of the drum kit. Ringo – usually addressed as Ritchie by his bandmates – was becoming increasingly dissatisfied with his own playing, as well as feeling under-appreciated by and distanced from the others. He left the group and walked out – becoming the first member ever to leave The Beatles of his own volition – and took his family for a two-week break in Sardinia. People at the studio were sworn to secrecy, so the media didn't get a whiff of the story.

The remaining Beatles soldiered on without him, recording the song with all three taking turns on the drums. While on holiday, Ringo relaxed on the comedian Peter Sellers' yacht, where he ordered fish and chips; the chips arrived, but instead of the fish there was squid, which he'd never tried before. After a conversation with the vessel's captain about octopuses, and their habit of collecting stones and other objects from the seabed to make underwater "gardens", Ringo was inspired to begin writing the song 'Octopus's Garden'.

When their new single 'Hey Jude' was released on August 30, The Beatles had become – unbeknown to most of the world – a trio. But their flattering "please come home" message to Ringo had the desired effect, and the drummer returned on Tuesday, September 3, to find his kit swathed in bright flowers. They spent the afternoon and evening of the following day at Twickenham Film Studios, where they made promotional films for 'Hey Jude' and its B-side, 'Revolution', directed by Michael Lindsay-Hogg. Born to an American actress and an English baronet, Sir Michael had worked in Irish television before landing a job as director on the British TV pop show *Ready Steady Go!* in the mid-sixties. He went on to become a "video" pioneer, making promotional films for The Rolling Stones as well as The Beatles, and had previously worked with the Fab Four in 1966, directing their promos for the single 'Paperback Writer' and its flipside, 'Rain'.

For the new promos, 'Hey Jude' and 'Revolution' were given a conventional presentation, with the group playing together on stage, backed by a 36-piece orchestra and watched by an audience of 300 extras, who joined in with the joyful "la-la-la-lah" coda to 'Hey Jude'. There were no psychedelic costumes, as there had been for their 'Hello, Goodbye' promo the previous year, and no surrealistic larking about, as there had been for 'Strawberry Fields Forever'. Despite being asked to do 12 takes and having to work into the early hours of the next morning, The Beatles found the experience enjoyable, and Michael watched with interest as they relaxed between takes and casually performed snatches of other songs. The broadcaster David Frost arrived to film an introduction for his television show, in which he called them "the greatest tea-room orchestra in the world" and declared that this was "their first live appearance for goodness knows how long" – although, in fact, only their vocals were performed live. Cliff Richard also got in on the act, filming an introduction for his own TV show.

As 'Hey Jude' rocketed up the singles charts, Paul talked to *Melody Maker* about the promos. "We decided to do clips this time, instead of zany films and that sort of thing," he said. "We all really enjoyed doing it." The Beatles watched the final edits of the films with Denis O'Dell, at which point an idea was tossed around and approved by everybody: wouldn't it be great if they made another film of some kind? Not just another promo, but something longer.

But for the time being it was back to the studio, as The Beatles continued to immerse themselves in the White Album. On September 6, Eric Clapton arrived at Abbey Road to lay down lead guitar on George's song 'While My Guitar Gently Weeps'. He had initially refused George's request, saying: "Nobody plays on a Beatles record." Of course, the guitarist was forgetting a host of people, including the string quartet on 'Yesterday', the Indian musicians on 'Within You Without You', and the orchestra on 'A Day In The Life', not to mention their producer George Martin, who played piano on several Beatles tracks.

That Friday and Saturday, The Doors and Jefferson Airplane played at the Roundhouse, the former train-engine shed in Chalk Farm, north London, that had been revitalised as a music venue. When Doors singer Jim Morrison saw the building for the first time, he said: "This is going to be fun. This is the place for us." It turned out to be the only London venue his band would ever play.

The Beatles still had another month of studio work to do on the White Album, and this certainly wasn't their most convivial recording experience. Individual members of the group spent many hours on their own compositions, and at times John and Paul would be recording different songs in separate rooms. Tensions were ramped up by John's insistence that Yoko attend many of the sessions. Nevertheless, Paul maintained an optimistic view of the group's future, and was already conceiving their next project. He was excited enough to spill some details to the music papers. "We will be doing a live TV show later in the year," he announced. "I don't know about a concert, but it might lead to that. I love the idea of playing again, and I know the others feel the same way." It had been two full years since their final concert at Candlestick Park in San Francisco, and Paul still had the setlist taped to the Höfner violin bass he had played there. "The idea of singing live is much more appealing now," he said. "We are beginning to miss it."

On September 21, when the jazz giant Ray Charles performed at the Royal Festival Hall on London's South Bank, George Harrison and his friend Eric Clapton were in the audience. Before Ray came on stage, the keyboard player from his band entertained the crowd with some organ-playing and singing. He broke into 'Agent Double O Soul', the Edwin Starr song about a funky James Bond-style spy, performing some leg-shaking, arm-shaking dance moves in the instrumental sections. George recognised him: "I thought, 'That guy looks familiar,' but he seemed bigger than I remembered. After a while, Ray came on and the band played for a few songs and then he reintroduced... Billy Preston!" The announcement confirmed that this was indeed an old friend of The Beatles.

Billy had met them during their nightclub performances in Hamburg in 1962. The Beatles would open for the rock'n'roll star Little Richard, whose band included Billy on organ. Billy would enjoy standing in the wings and watching The Beatles perform; one night, George even suggested he join them on organ, but Billy refused, fearing it would upset Little Richard if The Beatles borrowed a member of his band. Now, reacquainted seven years later with the Texan-born musician's mastery of the keyboard, George filed the memory of the concert away for later reflection.

In the meantime, the London waxwork attraction Madame Tussaud's updated its figures of The Beatles to reflect their latest hairstyles and taste in clothing. It was the fifth time in four years that technicians had given their effigies a makeover. A few days later, the curtain rose on an exciting new production at the Shaftesbury Theatre in the West End of London. This was *Hair*, a musical about hippies, free love and the Vietnam War. The show had opened earlier in the year on Broadway in New York, and was already notorious for its onstage nudity.

The morning after *Hair* opened, 'Hey Jude' hit number one in Britain, where it would linger for the next nine weeks. Nevertheless, there were still financial worries at Apple, which was widely perceived as a business that couldn't survive for very much longer. The technical engineer Dave Harries, who worked for EMI and had helped The Beatles with many of their recordings, was asked if he wanted to leave EMI and become an Apple employee. Interviewed by George Harrison, he asked if Apple could double his EMI salary of £2,000 per annum. When George asked him why he wanted so much money – £4,000 a year – Dave replied that he thought the move would be risky, because EMI would probably continue forever, whereas Apple might not. He didn't get the job.

Wanting a firmer hand on the tiller, The Beatles looked around for the ideal person to rescue their struggling company. They had a meeting with Lord Beeching, the man who had taken an axe to Britain's railway system five years before, leading to the closure of many "uneconomic" lines and stations. Beeching didn't want the Apple job, and his parting advice was that the group should concentrate on their music.

'Hey Jude' was still sitting at the top of the charts and receiving considerable radio play when, on the morning of Friday, October 18, John and Yoko received a surprise visit from the Metropolitan Police. They were lying in bed at Ringo's flat in Montagu Square – where they were living temporarily – when they heard a disturbance outside. After the police banged on the window and pushed at the door, several officers were eventually admitted to the flat. Dogs were brought in, sniffing out more than 200 grains of cannabis resin, and John and Yoko were taken to Paddington Green police station and charged with possession of drugs and obstruction. The police might have found a lot more had John and Yoko not been warned of the raid a few weeks in advance by a journalist friend and removed most of their narcotics from the flat.

The notorious Detective Sergeant Pilcher had commanded the raid. At that time, 33-year-old Norman "Nobby" Pilcher of the Drug Squad was advancing his career and getting his kicks by busting famous pop stars. His other victims included Donovan and members of The Rolling Stones. But this time his overzealousness had been noticed: the home secretary, James Callaghan, questioned the necessity for so many police officers and dogs in a raid on just two people, and asked him how the press had managed to arrive so promptly on the scene.

George and his wife Pattie were having a much better time than John and Yoko. They had flown to the USA with The Beatles' old friend and road manager Mal Evans in order to accompany one of Apple's recording artists, the singer Jackie Lomax, on a promotional tour of various cities. This became an extended trip of nearly seven weeks when George decided to book time at Sound Recorders Studio in Hollywood to finish recording Jackie's debut album, *Sour Milk Sea*. George also found time to socialise with Donovan, Frank Sinatra and members of Cream, and to play music with Bob Dylan at his house in Bearsville, near Woodstock in New York. The pair wrote the song 'I'd Have You Anytime', which would become the opening track of *All Things Must Pass*.

At the end of October, the photographer Linda Eastman moved in with Paul at his house in Cavendish Avenue, along with Heather, her five-year-old daughter from her severed 1962 marriage to geologist Joseph Melville See. Paul and Linda had originally met on May 15, 1967, at the Bag O'Nails club in

London's West End, after being introduced by Peter Brown – although Paul and Jane Asher were still an item then, and would remain so for more than a year.

"I knew Linda because she'd been married before and lived in Arizona," says Peter, "and when they broke up she came back to New York with her daughter and wanted to be a photographer. And she did not want to be an Eastman, all that Park Avenue stuff: she didn't think that was cool. So she became friendly with a little group of gay men, who I was part of. She decided that this group of guys was very cool, and she became part of the group. So I became friendly with her and I liked her a lot.

"When she came to London once, she came to see me at the office with her portfolio. And the only thing that was in the portfolio was a lot of photographs taken in New York of The Rolling Stones. I told her I didn't have time to look at it then, but could she leave it with me? She did, and I went through it and I loved the pictures. She came to pick it up and I said I'd taken one out – 'I'm sure you've got plenty of them and you don't mind me taking one out, because I'd like to keep it.' And she said, 'The one of Brian Jones.' And I said, 'How would you know which one I took?' It was one of Brian on his own. And she said she just knew. I loved Brian and we were very good friends, but she didn't know that. So I really took to her: I loved her, I thought she was savvy, and we became friends."

On May 15, 1967, Peter called in at Abbey Road studios. "And Paul was there on his own, finishing something or other, and then he said to me, 'What are you doing later?' I said, 'Nothing.' And he said 'Well, hang on a bit and we'll go and get some dinner.' So we went to the Bag O'Nails club for dinner, which is where Linda, who I knew from New York, came over to say hello to me and I introduced her to Paul."

Yoko was expecting her first baby with John, which was due in February. But on November 4, suffering symptoms of stress, she was admitted to Queen Charlotte's Hospital in London. John kept a vigil in the hospital ward, sleeping beside her. When a bed was available he slept in it; otherwise he lay on the floor.

During their stay, John's divorce from Cynthia became official, and John and Yoko's experimental album *Unfinished Music No. 1: Two Virgins* was released in the USA. The grooves contained tape loops and ad-lib conversations, while the cover, a full-frontal naked selfie of the two soul mates taken in the flat in Montagu Square, was even more problematic for America, where it was concealed by a brown paper sleeve.

While in hospital, John and Yoko continued to make recordings, capturing the sound of their son's heartbeat in the womb. Tragically, on November 21, Yoko suffered a miscarriage, the cause of which appeared to be the distress caused by the recent dope bust. A week later, the day before *Two Virgins* came out in the UK, John pleaded guilty in court to possession of cannabis, and was fined £150 plus costs.

On November 5, 1968, the Republican challenger Richard Nixon narrowly defeated the vice-president, Hubert Humphrey, by half a million votes to become the 37th president of the USA, succeeding Lyndon B. Johnson. "Tricky Dick" was promising "law and order" in America and "peace with honour" in Vietnam, claiming he had a secret plan to bring the war to an end.

Michael Lindsay-Hogg was working with The Rolling Stones, preparing a colourful television special that would be known as *The Rolling Stones Rock And Roll Circus*. But he found the time to visit Apple in Savile Row after receiving a telephone call from Paul McCartney. Paul said The Beatles had been happy with his 'Hey Jude' and 'Revolution' promos, and now they wanted to make their own TV special and would like him to direct it.

Paul was talking about The Beatles making a departure from their customary working methods: instead of continually overdubbing to create complex masterpieces in the studio, they would get back to being a proper band again, recording a series of songs live with no tinkering or trickery – "no electronic whatchamacallit", as he later put it. A decision was made to sideline the group's long-serving record producer, George Martin, whom they associated with their more elaborate recordings. So Paul approached Glyn Johns, a record producer who was also part of the team on *Rock And Roll Circus*, asking him to engineer the sound for The Beatles' TV programme.

Apple was now considering possible gig venues for the recording of the TV special. Rather than playing a single concert, they might play up to three and have the best footage edited together. The group could be supported by some of the acts recently signed to their Apple label, such as the singers James Taylor, Mary Hopkin and Jackie Lomax. One obvious location was the Royal Albert Hall, where Cream had played their farewell bash towards the end of November. That was later dismissed, according to the *New Musical Express*, "because of booking and other problems".

Another contender was the Roundhouse, where The Doors and Jefferson Airplane had played in September. It had also hosted various hippie gigs and freak-outs, such as the launch party for the alternative newspaper *International Times* – an event Paul McCartney attended incognito, disguised as an Arab. Dates around the middle of December were set aside at the Roundhouse, and the event made the news in *NME*, which said there would be three live concerts there, with The Beatles performing songs from their new double album. The shows would benefit charity, and Mary Hopkin and Jackie Lomax would perform as well. "These concerts will be a mindbender," Apple executive Jeremy Banks told the paper. Alas, the Roundhouse concerts didn't materialise either.

Denis O'Dell took John and Paul to see a disused flour mill that he had discovered years before near the River Thames, but they turned that down as well. Denis complained that it was impossible to negotiate with The Beatles at that stage, because the members of the band were only ever in agreement about a location for a day or two at the most, before arbitrary differences developed between them.

The idea of playing on a big cruise liner was considered, but there were problems with the obvious contenders. The *Queen Elizabeth* had been sold to a group of American businessmen who wanted to keep it in Florida as a tourist attraction, and the new £30 million vessel *Queen Elizabeth 2* was still being tested and not ready for service. The *QE2* had serious engine trouble when it was trialled in the Atlantic over Christmas of 1968, with 750 brave "guinea pig" passengers on board.

One of Paul's ideas was that The Beatles return to Germany and play a club incognito, under the name of Rikki & The Red Streaks, to give people the surprise of their lives when they walked in. He hadn't dreamed up the name: it was a real group, early-sixties contemporaries of The Beatles in Liverpool and Hamburg. This was yet another idea that they didn't pursue, though Paul tucked it away for later in his career. After he formed Wings in the seventies, he took the band out to play low-profile, little-publicised college dates, eliciting those astounded looks when people realised they were in the presence of a Beatle. And the Wings single 'Seaside Woman', featuring Linda McCartney on lead vocals, was released under the similar pseudonym Suzy and The Red Stripes.

November 1968 ended with the release of an intriguing film: *Sympathy For The Devil*, directed by Jean-Luc Godard, which featured scenes of The Rolling Stones working on their *Beggars Banquet* album at London's Olympic Studios, intercut with other sequences about Black Power activism and pornography. Its original title, which it retained for its release on the continent, was *One Plus One*, the name suggested by Denis O'Dell for Godard's projected Beatles documentary. Reviewers were less than impressed with the movie, one calling it "boring, disjointed, distasteful and lacking in musical or narrative content".

Early in December, Elvis Presley's TV spectacular – now known as his Comeback Special – was broadcast on NBC in America, and was an enormous success, pulling in almost half the TV viewers in the USA. Dressed in black leather, the 33-year-old King of Rock'n'Roll redeemed himself by performing live on stage for the first time since 1961, and sounding vital and exciting again. For the "informal jam" sequence of the show, the singer sat in a circle with musicians including guitarist Scotty Moore and drummer DJ Fontana (keeping time on a guitar case) and belted out classics such as 'That's All Right Mama', 'Heartbreak Hotel', 'Blue Suede Shoes' and 'Lawdy Miss Clawdy'.

TV specials were very much the thing at the end of 1968. The December issue of *The Beatles Book Monthly* excited fans with the news that the details of the group's own "one-hour colour television show" would be announced shortly: "After rehearsals they will give a set of separate 'live' performances before invited audiences. All three shows will be recorded on colour videotape and the final television programme will be made up from the best parts of the three. Much of the material will be songs from the Beatles' current bundle of 30 LP tracks but a few oldies will be included too. Songs selected for each of the three performances may vary slightly. At press time nobody at Apple could say for sure whether or not a late decision would be made to include guest appearances by other Apple recording artists such as Mary Hopkin and Jackie Lomax."

The TV show, said the fan magazine, would eventually be seen "on a hundred million television screens all around the world". People were asked to stop deluging the Apple offices with letters requesting tickets for the shows: these letters already numbered more than 20,000, easily exceeding the number of available seats. But fans had a chance of attending if they entered *The Beatles Book Monthly*'s lucky dip, filling in a coupon and posting it to the magazine's London address; all the coupons would go into a big revolving drum, and a pair of tickets would be awarded for each of the first 50 coupons pulled out.

The news that they would be playing live again, said the magazine, "gives a very firm answer to those people who think that The Beatles want to retire from the rough and tumble of show business. They may get fed up with some of its worst aspects – and say so – leading people to believe that they will never, under any circumstances, do a certain thing again. But, they find a way round it because they don't really want to disappoint all the people who have supported them so well over the past few years." The magazine staff appeared to be drunk on optimism, asking fans who were lucky enough to receive tickets to write about the shows they saw. "We'll print a full selection of readers' letters about the Beatles' first 'live' performances for almost three years in a future issue."

In early December, John made home cassette recordings of himself as he composed new songs, singing in an appealingly rough and sleepy voice and playing acoustic guitar. The most repetitive of these began with the line "Everyone had a hard year" against a pattern of guitar-picking. In these early lyrics, everyone "had a good time" and "saw the sun shine", as well as having a "facelift". He was also riffing on colloquial expressions for behaviour, so everyone "let their hair down", "pulled their socks up" and "put their foot down". The song in this early, monotonous form was crying out for some development (such as a chorus, unless this *was* the chorus, repeated over and over again – in which case it needed verses). Fortunately, it was destined to be merged with Paul McCartney's 'I've Got A Feeling', where it somehow worked with miraculous perfection.

The other song was an early form of 'Don't Let Me Down', although it lacked a chorus and those title words didn't appear. But he was singing "I'm in love for the first time", and the stylish, Lennonesque false stops and unaccompanied introduction to the verse ("And if somebody loves you like she do...") were already there, as were the lines "It's a love that lasts forever/It's a love that has no past." It was clearly and unashamedly about his love for Yoko Ono.

Following *Sympathy For The Devil*, Jean-Luc Godard set about making a radical new film in America. For one scene in his movie, he filmed Jefferson Airplane on top of the Schuyler Hotel in the Midtown district of New York City. Grace Slick and the rest of the band ascended to the roof of the nine-storey building on 45th Street during the chilly afternoon of December 7, 1968. "Hello, New York!" cried the singer Marty Balin. "Wake up, you fuckers! Free music! Nice songs! Free love!"

They played a spirited version of their song 'The House At Pooneil Corners', succeeding in disrupting the flow of traffic in the streets below. But they were prevented from playing any more by the NYPD, who quickly intervened. One of the policemen offered a conflicted opinion of the event: "I don't mind – it's nice, believe me," he said. "It's a good change. But the city can't stand it. I can't either." The Airplane called a halt to their performance, and the actor Rip Torn, who was starring in Godard's film, was arrested for harassing an officer.

The 28-year-old Conservative councillor and fundraiser Jeffrey Archer paid a visit to Apple Corps, wanting a slice of the action after hearing rumours that The Beatles were planning a spectacular charity concert. Archer had met The Beatles back in March 1964 when he attended Brasenose College in Oxford, and he was photographed with the group after he obtained their support for an Oxfam campaign. At the time, Ringo remarked to the critic Sheridan Morley that he thought Archer was "the kind of bloke who would bottle your piss and sell it".

On December 10, the production of *The Rolling Stones Rock And Roll Circus* began at Wembley Studios in London. The project put an array of contemporary rock talent together, including the Stones, The Who and Eric Clapton, who was brought in to accompany John and Yoko. As circus performers swung and cavorted and Michael Lindsay-Hogg directed and Glyn Johns recorded, The Who played their song-cycle 'A Quick One While He's Away' and, early in the morning of December 11, the Stones played lacklustre versions of six songs, including 'Jumpin' Jack Flash' and 'Sympathy For The Devil'. There was one song apiece from Jethro Tull, Taj Mahal and Marianne Faithfull, and a short-lived supergroup called Dirty Mac – comprising John, Yoko, Eric, the Stones' Keith Richards on bass and Hendrix's drummer Mitch Mitchell – performed John's 'Yer Blues' from the White Album, plus a jam they called 'A Whole Lotta Yoko'.

A week later, John and Yoko continued to develop their embryonic career as artistic collaborators, performing at an alternative Christmas event staged at the Royal Albert Hall by the Arts Lab, an avant-garde organisation based in a London warehouse. The couple entered a large white bag on the stage, in which they remained for more than half an hour. That evening also saw a young woman in the audience spontaneously remove her clothes and dance around naked. When the authorities moved in to eject her, other free spirits began stripping off to show their solidarity.

Michael Lindsay-Hogg would attend a series of other meetings at Apple about The Beatles' own proposed TV special, though he was concerned that the other members of the group were displaying less commitment towards the project than Paul. Paul was so keen on it that he suggested an expansion of the concept: if Michael filmed the group during rehearsals, they could use the footage to make a 30-minute programme to be shown a week before the TV special, as a teaser.

Everybody agreed on a start date of early January 1969 for the filming, before the meeting ended with John Lennon playing a cassette. As Michael and the other Beatles listened attentively, the faint sounds that came out of the tape machine were of a man and woman talking intimately, giggling and making other, more suggestive noises. It soon became embarrassingly clear that it was a recording of John and Yoko having sex.

Across the Atlantic, three American astronauts prepared to make history. NASA's pioneering Apollo 8 mission would take Frank Borman, James Lovell and Bill Anders out of the Earth's orbit, round the moon 10 times, and back to Earth again. The day before blast-off, there were concerns that the weather might cause the flight to be postponed: the forecasters were predicting thick cloud and fog, and dense cloud would prevent visual tracking of the rocket up to 2,000 feet. In the event, the launch went ahead at the Kennedy Space Center in Florida on December 21, and the astronauts began their three-day approach to the moon.

Down on Earth, in Savile Row, the staff at Apple were expecting some unusual visitors. During his trip to California, George Harrison had met several Hells Angels, who told him they would be coming to London and paying him a call. George had already warned Apple staff about the rebel bikers in a memo, writing: "They will be twelve in number complete with black leather jackets and motor cycles. They will undoubtedly arrive at Apple and I have heard they may try to make full use of Apple's facilities. They may look as though they are going to do you in but are very straight and do good things, so don't fear them or up-tight them. Try to assist them without neglecting your Apple business and without letting them take control of Savile Row."

Only two Angels turned up, Frisco Pete and Billy Tumbleweed, but they and their roaring Harley-Davidsons quickly made an impression on the Mayfair street. The receptionist Debbie Wellum was one of many Apple staff who were transfixed by their dramatic arrival: "There was a heck of a noise outside, and they parked up in Savile Row and walked in, and the stench of patchouli oil was incredible."

As George had predicted, they made "full use of Apple's facilities", staying in a room in the building. They also raised the noise levels in the neighbourhood. "They were racing each other on their bikes," says Debbie, "and they'd go from the top of Savile Row, the Vigo Street end, all the way down to West End Central police station, screech to a halt, turn round and go back again and screech to a halt again. They knew it was a police station – I told them – but they didn't care. They tried to get me to go on the back of a motorbike with them, and I wouldn't go."

On Monday, December 23, Apple threw a big Christmas party which was attended by John and Yoko dressed as Father and Mother Christmas. The Hells Angels got into the spirit as well. "We had lovely food, laid on by Prudence and Primrose from the kitchen," says Debbie. "Prudence and Primrose were two very well-to-do *cordon-bleu* cooks who worked at Apple, and they cooked wonderful meals and were very good fun." One of the highlights of the day was the arrival on a tray of an enormous roast turkey. "When they laid all the food out, the Hells Angels walked in and started eating it. And when Prudence, the tiny one, asked if they would leave the food alone – because it wasn't time to eat it yet – they started picking it up and throwing it all round the place. I think they brought with them a lot of medication, shall we say, which they put in the punch."

The American Apple staffer Chris O'Dell, who worked in the A&R department, remembers a fight breaking out at the party between the Angels and *New Musical Express* journalist Alan Smith, whose wife, Mavis, assisted Derek Taylor in the press office. "I think the Hells Angels were drunk, for one thing, and they could just become obnoxious. And this reporter made a comment that pissed them off, so they just slugged him."

Frisco Pete and Billy Tumbleweed outstayed their welcome in the Apple building for a little longer, resisting a polite request from Neil Aspinall that they should leave, and it was left to George, who had sanctioned their visit in the first place, to give them their marching orders.

On Christmas Eve, as the crew of Apollo 8 orbited the moon, they made a live television broadcast, showing their views of the Earth and the moon and reading verses from the Book of Genesis. The broadcast was watched by millions, proving even more popular than Elvis' Comeback Special. Two days after Christmas Day, the latest American space heroes splashed down in the Pacific Ocean after their week-long adventure, becoming *Time* magazine's "Men of the Year". Dr Thomas Paine, acting director of NASA, declared: "I call this a triumph for the 'squares' of this world, the men who are not hippies and who work with slide rules, and are not ashamed to say a prayer."

The Beatles, if it were possible, were actually getting hairier. Paul had grown an impressive beard, and the recently altered waxworks at Madame Tussaud's were already out of date.

The Beatles' next big project, beginning with their rehearsals in front of the cameras and ending with their first live performance in more than two years, was now approaching rapidly. John, Paul,

George and Ringo enjoyed several days of peace and quiet over the remainder of Christmas and New Year, before reconvening in January 1969 to begin the most challenging and unpleasant period in their collective career.

CHAPTER TWO

Winter Blues

As the year 1968 gave way to 1969, George Harrison was in an upbeat mood. He was sharing his house – Kinfauns in Esher, Surrey – with not one but two very attractive women. There was Pattie, his wife of nearly three years; but there was also her friend Charlotte Martin, a Parisian model. Charlotte had recently split up with Eric Clapton, and she had been welcomed into the Harrison household to help her recover from the break-up.

There was an intriguing romantic complexity to this situation. One of the reasons why Eric had ended his relationship with Charlotte was his powerful attraction to George's wife, but George and Charlotte had recently begun an affair.

Putting his domestic concerns behind him, George was in creative mode on that first day of January, and he left the house to drive into London, walking into the Apple building at 3 Savile Row. A conversation shortly afterwards with The Beatles' publicist, Derek Taylor, set George thinking about a project that might have kept him busy for months. Taylor was a bright, funny, personable man who was respected by all four Beatles, and whose eccentric habits included addressing other men as "squire" or "vicar".

The artist Alan Aldridge once said of him: "You fell in love with this guy right away: warm, witty, urbane and full of hilarious repartee." On that New Year's Day, Derek suggested to George that the pair of them co-write a musical, the subject matter of which would be everyday life at Apple Corps. In the months since its inception, the company had quickly become a crazy, diverting adventure, full of colour and way-out ideas, and the publicist thought it was a promising basis for an all-singing, all-dancing extravaganza.

Days later, he explained the thinking behind the idea, the seed of which had come from a conversation with Mike Connor, head of the Apple offices in Los Angeles. "For everyone at Apple, life is a mixture of fact and fiction," said Derek. "Often this office is like *Alice In Wonderland*, and, since Apple is constantly surrounded and involved in music, it seemed a natural subject to base a musical around. George has already written an outline and some of the music. I'm in charge of ideas and lyrics."

George was a good choice for musical collaborator. Not only had he produced the *Sour Milk Sea* album for Jackie Lomax and jammed with Bob Dylan, but also his soundtrack to the film *Wonderwall* – on which he worked with various Indian musicians – had recently hit the record shelves. He was behaving for all the world like a free and easy solo songwriter and producer, almost forgetting – perhaps deliberately – that he was still under contract as a member of the world's most successful pop group, and that it was very nearly time to work on The Beatles' next project. On the following day, January 2, he was expected to join his bandmates at one of their old haunts, Twickenham Film Studios, to begin rehearsals.

These were not regular rehearsals, hence the movie-studio location. As Paul McCartney had suggested towards the end of the year, they would be filmed, and the footage would be edited and used to promote their forthcoming TV special.

Twickenham Film Studios, a discreet cluster of buildings over the road from St Margarets railway station in Twickenham, was The Beatles' default movie-making facilities. This was where they had shot the non-location scenes for their first two films, *A Hard Day's Night* and *Help!*; they had made promotional films here in 1965 for the songs 'I Feel Fine', 'Ticket To Ride', 'Help!', 'Day Tripper' and 'We Can Work It Out', as well as for 'Hey Jude' and 'Revolution' in September 1968. For The Beatles' colleagues at Apple, including Neil Aspinall and Denis O'Dell, it seemed the obvious place to make a new film.

But the promos had been relatively short, and the big movies had been quite tightly directed, with the members of the group playing versions of themselves fleshed out by scriptwriters. This time it was *cinéma vérité*: they *were* themselves on screen, and there was no script.

The Beatles had certainly been in situations before where the outcome of a project was uncertain. On a small scale, individual songs with fairly ordinary beginnings had blossomed into sonic masterworks in the studio: 'Strawberry Fields Forever', say, or 'Tomorrow Never Knows'. On a larger scale, *Magical Mystery Tour* had grown from a vague idea about a psychedelic coach trip into a daring and controversial TV film, plus a series of excellent songs. But this latest project seemed especially open-ended, and its ultimate medium amorphous; and on top of that, the group was not in the best of collective health.

It was less than three months since they had finished work on the White Album, which they had packed with original compositions, draining their collective stock of musical ideas. And now John and Ringo, like George, had their own extracurricular projects to occupy them. John's relationship with Yoko Ono was intense and virtually all-consuming, and the couple had already begun their career of international political agitation. Ringo was looking forward to an acting job in *The Magic Christian*, a new comedy film directed by his friend Peter Sellers in which the drummer played a homeless orphan adopted by Sellers' character, the billionaire Sir Guy Grand. The movie looked like the start of a new career for Ringo, and provided a hard deadline for The Beatles' latest project, as he was scheduled to arrive for hair and make-up in February.

A more damaging and disruptive factor at The Beatles' Twickenham sessions was heroin, which had entered John and Yoko's lives the previous year. This was a particular worry for Paul, who later remembered that John "was getting into harder drugs than we'd been into, and so his songs were taking on more references to heroin. Until that point we had made rather mild, rather oblique references to pot or LSD. Now John started to be talking about fixes and monkeys, and it was a harder terminology which the rest of us weren't into. We were disappointed that he was getting into heroin because we didn't really see how we could help him. We just hoped it wouldn't go too far."

John later ascribed his and Yoko's opiate usage to the criticism and mockery to which the pair were subjected by the outside world, and within the group itself. "I never injected it or anything," he told *Rolling Stone* in 1970. "We sniffed a little when we were in real pain. And we get into so much pain that we have to do something about it. And that's what happened to us. We took 'H' because of what The Beatles and others were doing to us."

But what heroin was doing to Lennon, a once-prolific songwriter who had been the *de facto* leader of The Beatles in their early days, was anything but conducive to the intensive work required by the new project. It evidently dulled his creativity and made him lazy and lethargic, and it would trigger conflict within The Beatles as they progressed with the project that would become *Let It Be*.

The only group member who appeared to be 100% committed to the filmed rehearsals was Paul, who had initiated them in the first place. On one level, he was clearly concerned that The Beatles were disintegrating, and believed that a collective project of some kind, perhaps any kind, would give them the cohesion and enthusiasm they needed to survive as a unit. On another level, his innate work ethic continually demanded that he remain occupied. Several years later, he told an interviewer: "One of my hang-ups has always been having a job. With *Let It Be*, I remember us having a meeting and me saying I wanted to do a film, and John saying, 'Oh, I *see*, he wants a job. He wants work.' And I did. We hadn't done anything for three months and I was getting a bit itchy."

This was the general pattern after the death of their manager, Brian Epstein, in August 1967: without any spoken agreement, McCartney would take up the mantle of marshalling the group for their next project, like a stern father mobilising his bone-idle teenage sons to do *something* with their lives, for Christ's sake.

"From Brian's death onwards, Paul was always the driving force," recalls Peter Brown, "because he was the one who had the energy and wanted to get on with things. *Magical Mystery Tour* was the first of those things. And although Paul could be irritating, he was enormously helpful to me, because putting Apple together was not easy.

"Although The Beatles were the owners, Neil Aspinall and I were on the board. But still my attitude was to get anything done, we had to have the approval of The Beatles, obviously. And it was only Paul who would be willing to come in and discuss things. At that point he was the only one who lived in London. Ringo had an apartment in London, but he didn't really live there. I would call Paul and say, 'Will you come in? We need to sit down and talk,' and he would. Also, it wasn't just because he was in London: it was because he was the one who had all that energy."

Back in 1967, Peter had witnessed Paul's strength as a motivator, which was evident even in times of trouble. "When they stopped touring, for the first time in their career they had lots of time to go into the studio if they wanted to. *Sgt. Pepper*, which is one of the greatest albums of all time, was made over several months... So there was a sort of relaxation in the summer of '67, and then Brian died, and Paul's attitude was 'What are we gonna do now?' And I remember being very irritated myself, because it was very upsetting for me when Brian died, because he was my best friend as well as my colleague. And then also I had to be the prime witness in the coroner's court, which was very harrowing, then I went to Liverpool for the funeral. We asked The Beatles not to come, because of the media and everything. We did it very fast, before anyone thought the funeral was going to take place, and then the moment I got back, Paul decided that we had to have a meeting. We did it in Ringo's apartment in Montagu Square. The meeting was between all The Beatles, Neil and Mal and me, and I was really depressed and miserable, and not very keen to be doing this so quickly, like within a couple of days of the funeral, but Paul insisted on it.

"I was sort of chairing that meeting and I wasn't feeling great, and then we took a coffee break and I got up and walked across the room, and I was looking through the window, into space. And then I suddenly felt these arms around me from the back, hugging me, and someone saying, 'Are you all right?' It was John. And I turned round and said, 'No, I'm not,' and he said, 'Nor am I.' I think one of the reasons that John and I got on together subsequent to Brian's death is that we both loved Brian. But my point is that Paul was determined that we should get on with business. The fact that Brian wasn't there any more was even more reason why we should do it and do it immediately, which is why *Magical Mystery Tour* happened so quickly."

From that first week of January 1969, The Beatles essentially became commuters, travelling daily from their homes to the film studio, putting in several hours of rehearsal, and returning home in the late afternoon or the evening. John, George and Ringo were all coming by road from different towns in Surrey, the most Beatle-infested county in the kingdom. George was coming in from Esher, about six miles away, taking him little over a quarter of an hour on a good day. Ringo had the longest journey of them all, whizzing in from Brookfields, his new home in Elstead, 25 miles away in the south-western part of the county, which would have taken up to an hour. At that time, John and Yoko were living eight miles from Twickenham in Ringo's previous residence, Sunny Heights in Weybridge, which the drummer had yet to sell; their journey would have taken about half an hour.

Paul's main home was in Cavendish Avenue, a tree-lined street of substantial houses tucked away behind Lord's Cricket Ground in St John's Wood, just a short zip from Abbey Road and about 12 miles from Twickenham. Unlike the others, and despite his status as one of the world's most famous pop idols, Paul would often use public transport between north London and Twickenham. The Beatles' assistant Mal Evans described Paul's journey on that first day, Thursday, January 2, for the amusement of fans:

"At half eight that morning, between bites of breakfast, I'd telephoned round all four fellows to remind them it was getting up time and they were due at Twickenham by eleven. On that first day Paul was last to arrive – half an hour after noon! – having come by underground, then local train, then taxi from Hampton Court station. He'd meant to do the entire journey by public transport but, knowing he was late, he chickened out and caught a cab rather than wait at the bus stop!"

The Beatle may have been concerned that he might be recognised and mobbed by fans at that Hampton Court bus stop, despite the fact that he had recently grown a bushy black beard that made him look a bit like a Cuban revolutionary. The previous year, he had dared to make several incognito journeys, employing a variety of attention-diverting costumes. Denis O'Dell was amused by the way McCartney and Linda Eastman managed to retain their privacy while moving around in New York City and Los Angeles, as well as London: "This was possible largely because throughout 1968 Paul had become a master of disguise. He greatly valued being able to do the things that most of us take for granted, such as taking a bus or walking in a park, and was not prepared to let his celebrity status prevent him from doing normal, everyday things. In an effort to retain his anonymity he had learned to dress and behave in a manner that would prevent him from being recognised. He managed to achieve this by wearing very ordinary clothes that seemed to come from a previous era. In fact some of them did. During that year he bought a great many garments secondhand from Portobello Market and frequently travelled to the Wigmore Street offices by bus. When I questioned him about his unconventional fashion sense, he replied, 'Denis, you have to understand, these are clothes that you can move about in.'"*

Like McCartney on that first day of filming, the other Beatles didn't always arrive on time for their rehearsal duties. Though their individual timekeeping was erratic, The Beatles nonetheless became everyday commuters at one of the worst times of the year, the middle of winter. The weather wasn't the main problem: in fact, January 1969 was an unusually mild month, thanks to a gentle airstream caressing England from the south-west. It was the shortness of the days: the fact that the sun didn't come up until around 8 a.m., but went down again as early as 4 p.m. At this time of year, many ordinary commuters know the misery of leaving their homes before sunrise and returning to them after sunset, as

---

* From *At The Apple's Core* by Denis O'Dell with Bob Neaverson.

each day's window of light is eclipsed by their hours in the workplace.

The Beatles would have suffered – more than many office and shop workers, who at least had windows to look out of – from daylight deprivation. The term "seasonal affective disorder" (SAD) had yet to be coined (it wasn't named in print until 1985) but these short days would likely have had a negative bearing on the musicians' wellbeing, mood and mental health. SAD is a form of depression, whose symptoms can include lethargy, anxiety and irritability.

Moreover, getting up every morning for work was not something to which they were accustomed, and would possibly have brought back unpleasant memories of their days as ordinary jobbing teenagers. Just 10 years before, John had briefly toiled as a labourer on a building site, which he loathed. Paul had once spent numbingly tedious days winding electrical coils, while George had worked as an apprentice electrician, and Ringo had been a railway delivery boy, a barman on a ferry and a trainee joiner.

The idea was still for The Beatles to develop new material for a series of concerts in a location that had yet to be decided. The concerts would be filmed for the TV special and recorded for a live album. "We went into the filming with no plan for where the concerts would take place," says Michael Lindsay-Hogg, "and the idea was that the plan would come as we talked and we all turned up at the soundstage on January 2nd."

That day at Twickenham, the group ran through no fewer than three of the new songs they would eventually play in the rooftop concert – though, of course, they had no idea then that they would be playing from the top of the Apple building. They sat in a huddle on the soundstage to play music – as Elvis and his band had done in the Comeback Special, and as members of The Rolling Stones had done in Godard's *Sympathy For The Devil*.

Before Paul arrived via his public-transport adventure, the others got off to a reasonable start, playing embryonic versions of Lennon's 'Don't Let Me Down' and 'Dig A Pony'. Other songs were performed that would have no place in the concert, and indeed would never properly be recorded by The Beatles as a group. These included George's poignant 'All Things Must Pass' and John's 'On The Road To Marrakesh'.*

Later, the whole group would tackle 'I've Got A Feeling', on which John and Paul had evidently collaborated before these rehearsals – Paul having written the main hook, and John contributing the "Everybody had a hard year" tune from his December cassette recording. By now they had become quite adept at fusing Lennon song fragments with McCartney fragments, as they had done with 'We Can Work It Out' (John adding the "Life is very short" middle section to Paul's jauntier verses and chorus), 'A Day In The Life' (Paul adding the section about getting out of bed) and 'Baby, You're A Rich Man' (Paul adding the chorus to Lennon's verses).

On that opening day of the sessions they complained about the cavernous space in which they were having to perform. This was Stage One, the studios' biggest soundstage – a spartan cuboid box 118 feet long and 64 feet wide, with a 34-foot-high ceiling. In happier days, they had filmed most of the interior scenes for *A Hard Day's Night* and *Help!* here. Today it was quite cold – recalling the site's earlier use as an ice rink – although occasionally they would receive bursts of heat from the lights suspended around them, illuminating the scene for the cameras.

Kevin Harrington, the 18-year-old red-haired Londoner who had helped Mal Evans see to The Beatles' everyday needs during

---

* Also known as 'Child Of Nature', this would eventually evolve into 'Jealous Guy' on his *Imagine* album.

the making of the White Album, could immediately see that this setting wasn't conducive to creativity and contentment. "It just didn't feel right," Kevin recalls now. "I'd spent months in this nice environment at Abbey Road, and then we were suddenly plonked in this aircraft hangar, with The Beatles in the middle and all these people around them, and they were under all this pressure to perform."

Paul Bond was 22 and the youngest member of the camera crew. "I was the clapper boy, spending a lot of the time loading and unloading films. But it was lovely to be working in January, because traditionally the film industry here doesn't work then. It was a month's work, plus we were working with The Beatles, so it was just heaven. I was Charlie Hot Potatoes to all the girls I knew. But the group were playing in this vast, empty space, and it seemed wrong."

There were consolations for George and Ringo, who had some shiny new equipment to play with. George had taken delivery of a new electric guitar, a Rosewood Telecaster custom-made for him by Fender in the USA, which had its own seat on the aircraft that transported it to London. Ringo had a new Ludwig Hollywood kit, with a maple finish, though he preferred to use an old Ludwig snare drum instead of the all-metal snare that came with the Hollywood kit. John was still playing the Epiphone Casino hollow-bodied electric guitar he had been using since the *Revolver* album, though during the recording of the White Album he had removed its sunburst finish; it had been sanded down to the bare wood, which had then been lacquered. Paul was playing a Blüthner piano and his old Höfner violin bass, which still had the setlist from Candlestick Park taped to it. During the sessions, he would remove a "Bassman" sticker from his bass speaker cabinet and whimsically affix it to his Höfner as well.

As the first day of rehearsals progressed, there were tentative discussions about the locations for the upcoming concerts they were expected to play. "We talked about it a bit, and they all had different ideas," says Michael. "I think Ringo had the idea to go back to the Cavern in Liverpool, where they'd played in the early days, and do the special there. But my feeling was that the world had changed so much since they'd started, and *their* world had changed so much, that it needed a bigger stage than that. And I'd heard about this amphitheatre on the coast of Tunisia. It may have been that I was talking to someone who was vacationing in that part of the world and said something about that amphitheatre. It could have been a friend, because at that period a lot of people in the rock'n'roll community, and the hippie community, were spending a lot of time in northern Africa – in places like Morocco and Algeria."

The building in question was the huge amphitheatre at the town of El Djem, near the coast of Tunisia, which was built by the Romans in the 3rd century AD. This was the setting for gladiatorial combat and chariot races in ancient times, and it could accommodate 35,000 seated spectators.

"It seemed to fit the bill for a variety of reasons: one, because it would be the world stage they were on, as opposed to just the Liverpudlian stage they were on, and because of the scale of the thing; and two, I also had these images of it starting at dawn, and the dawn in North Africa can be very beautiful. The stage would begin to be set up at dawn – I don't think The Beatles would be up at dawn, but it would be Mal or whoever would be setting up the stage – and then the sun would start to come up. That part of the world had a variety of people: Arabs, Muslims, Christians, black, white, but in any event we would make it a kind of melting pot, so when The Beatles began to play, the idea was that the music would start to float across the desert – an aerial shot would pull away from the desert and little musical notes would appear on the screen and fade into the distance, and from the distance would come a variety of people of all races and creeds – because The Beatles were ecumenical in their beliefs about how we should all get on. So by the end of the show, when it was dark and 10 or 11 o'clock at night, the idea was that the amphitheatre would be filled with the world. And so when they were playing 'Let It Be' or 'The Long And Winding Road', it would be the world and The Beatles, all together. That was my idea, which I still think is a pretty good one, actually."

But already the group showed little enthusiasm for a big overseas show, and Paul pointed out that Ringo had ruled out the idea of travelling abroad, not having enjoyed the food in India. At this point, even Paul seemed to favour the easy option of broadcasting their TV special from these Twickenham studios, with a finale of some kind staged here or at a smaller venue, or perhaps even outdoors.

Back they came to Twickenham on the second day. This time Paul was an early arrival, and he amused himself with some well-known tunes on the piano, including 'Tea For Two' and 'Chopsticks', before toying with the theme tune for *Torchy The Battery Boy* – a children's puppet drama series directed and co-produced by Gerry Anderson* and shown on Britain's ITV network between 1960 and 1961, during the formative years of The Beatles.

During that Friday, they managed some decent run-throughs of 'Don't Let Me Down' and 'I've Got A Feeling', with Paul leading them through the bluesy, screaming bridge, which they tried out on one occasion in two-part harmony. John was still adjusting his words for the "hard year" section, and everybody was having a

---

* More famous for later creations such as *Thunderbirds*.

"facelift", a "knees-up" and a "soft dream" — though he had begun using "wet dream" instead by now.

Paul was enthusing about the idea of being filmed like this as they refined new material. He likened it to a film about Picasso painting, in which the artist might start with a blank canvas and end up with a finished work — suggesting that they were also starting from nothing, but would end up with a priceless TV show.

They made more than a dozen attempts at George's 'All Things Must Pass', and played Paul's new song 'Maxwell's Silver Hammer', but there was a lot of fooling around as well, and they were continually drawn to old material — other people's songs, such as 'Hitch Hike', 'What Do You Want To Make Those Eyes At Me For?' and 'Piece Of My Heart', as well as songs from their own back catalogue, such as 'I'm So Tired' and 'Ob-La-Di, Ob-La-Da' from the White Album.

Every time they dropped their new songs and burst into an oldie, it was an act of procrastination: they were retreating from the task at hand, and lazily seeking solace in numbers they already knew and required no work. They would have been wise to the fact that the new material demanded discussions about how it should be arranged and played, creating the potential for conflict between them (which did actually happen several times during these sessions), while old songs could be dashed off casually and comfortably. And in the absence of a strict musical director, they were at liberty to hop haphazardly from one song to another at will, often leaving numbers unfinished. It certainly wasn't the best recipe for job satisfaction.

Their adoption of a loose, stripped-down sound — turning away from the overdubbed complexity of some of their mid-period work, such as *Sgt. Pepper's Lonely Hearts Club Band*, to make what John called "honest" recordings — was partly inspired by the music and working methods of The Band, the rootsy Canadian-American group that had released their debut album, *Music From Big Pink*, the year before. However, as George Harrison's biographer Graeme Thomson has pointed out, The Beatles' situation was a million miles from that of The Band's: "The parallels in reality were almost non-existent. The Band worked in a comfortable old wooden house in the Catskill Mountains, making music all day, playing American football in the yard and chess and cards in the living room, eating and drinking together. The warm, easy sound they made was a natural extension of their friendships and the lives they were living. The Beatles, by contrast, were recording in a sterile film studio and were finding it increasingly hard to be civil to one another. Not only that, they struggled to function as a band any more."

It must have occurred to The Beatles that less than nine months before, they had played in an environment that was the polar opposite of these studios. They had enjoyed sunny days and balmy evenings in Rishikesh, India, where they meditated and recited mantras with the Maharishi and sat around jamming blissfully on acoustic guitars. One of the Beatle wives who accompanied them, Pattie Boyd, paints a vivid picture of those days: "The environment was very inspiring, and Paul and John were in a very mellow mood, which was not always the case when they were songwriting in London. They were all on the same plane, and it became much easier for George to join in with them and write songs and not be rejected. They got on creatively really, really well in Rishikesh. We were there for a reason and it made everybody really mellow. Plus, I have to say – no drink or drugs. There was no outside stimulating interference, which was a major factor…"

Another major factor was that they hadn't been sent expressly to India to prepare for a musical project – although in the end, perhaps precisely because they were lacking that kind of career pressure, they wrote a heap of songs, many of which ended up on the White Album. In fact, when McCartney reverted to type in Rishikesh and started to plot The Beatles' next move, he was brought up short by Harrison. "George actually once got very annoyed and told me off," he remembered years later, "because I was trying to think of the next album. He said, 'We're not fucking here to do the next album, we're here to meditate.' It was like, 'Ooh excuse me for breathing!', you know. George was quite strict about that."

During their discussions in Twickenham, it emerged that there was a problem with the new material – apart from the fact that there wasn't that much of it. Both George and Paul admitted that many of the songs they had written were slow numbers, echoing John's complaint about his own songs the day before, when he had suggested they try to write some rockers.

One uptempo song that they played that day was new to most of the people around them – the film crew and the sound technicians – although it wasn't new to the group. 'One After 909' was a song begun by John as a teenager back in the late fifties: a juvenile homage to the American tradition of songs about trains, and to skiffle numbers like Lonnie Donegan's 'Rock Island Line'. The Beatles had recorded it at EMI back in 1963, but it hadn't been deemed good enough to release. Now they dusted it off, though they had reservations about the words.

"I never, sort of, knew what it was about before," admitted Paul. "So she's on a train and he, sort of…"

"He goes to the station and misses it," explained John.

"But he goes back and finds it was the wrong number," said Paul.

"Wrong location," said George.

"To rhyme with 'station', you know," said John.

Paul added that his brother, Mike, had been suggesting for years that The Beatles use the song. "But I said, 'Well, you know, Mike, you don't understand about these things, you know.'"

George made a case here for meaningless song lyrics. "Most people just don't give a shit what the words are about, as long as it's 'pop of the month'," he said. And John confessed that "we always thought it wasn't finished. We couldn't be bothered finishing it."

The song is certainly questionable. While the railway-flavoured lyrics fit the tune nicely as it chugs along, they don't make sense in the cold light of day. After the narrator's "baby" has informed him, perhaps with a deliberately cryptic vagueness, that she is taking the train behind the one scheduled for 9.09, he tells her to "move over, honey" because he is also "travelling on that line". The narrator runs to the station, laden with luggage, only to be informed by a "railman" that he's in the wrong place. We aren't told whether or not the railman was helpful enough to tell him where the right location is. Apparently not, because our hero then runs back home with his bags, and somehow discovers that he "got the number wrong". That's the end of the story, and we don't even know if his baby was travelling on the one after the 9.09 a.m. or after the 9.09 p.m., which would have made a considerable difference to his romantic plans.

Between rehearsing songs, John was making improvised quips, as he was wont to do, parodying the lyrics of songs such as 'Ob-La-Di, Ob-La-Da' ("Desmond had a sparrow in the parking lot") and composing humorous dedications to an imaginary audience. He pretended to have received a request from "the Cement Mixers' Guild", which was the actual name that a coterie of female Beatles fans had once given themselves.

The Beatles had only played for two days, and now they had the luxury of Saturday and Sunday off, which ought to have raised their spirits a little. Back home, George wrote a new gospel song, 'Hear Me Lord'. Paul, in a more retrospective frame of mind, put *Sgt. Pepper* on his turntable. They also watched some television.

The BBC had some interesting TV shows that weekend. Saturday evening brought *Happening For Lulu*, a variety showcase for the eponymous pop singer, broadcast from the corporation's Shepherd's Bush building and entailing a bit of singing, dancing and comedy plus some special guests. The *Daily Express*, which described Lulu as "that explosive little cracker from the Glasgow backstreets", warned that each show "will be informal and unscripted, with an audience of teenagers". The show was also live, so there was no telling what might happen. The guests that evening included The Jimi Hendrix Experience, performing 'Voodoo Chile' and a couple of minutes of 'Hey Joe' – at which point Jimi departed from the script.

"We're gonna stop playing this *rubbish*," he announced (you could almost hear the distant wailing from his public-relations team), "and dedicate a song to the Cream... I'd like to dedicate this to Eric Clapton, Ginger Baker and Jack Bruce." They immediately tore into a cover of Cream's 'Sunshine Of Your Love', which ended up crashing the sacred evening news slot and prompted the producers to take the show off air. The following week, the programme was billed simply as *Lulu*, the *Happening* no doubt dispensed with for fear of something similar occurring again.

Sunday evening saw footage of Cream themselves, in an *Omnibus* documentary directed by Tony Palmer that included part of their November 1968 farewell concert at the Royal Albert Hall. The programme hailed the now-defunct group as a revolutionary and ground-breaking force in popular music. "What Eric Clapton, Jack Bruce and Ginger Baker have done," said the narrator, "is to show the form of most pop music – eight-bar phrases, simple-minded harmonic progressions and nursery-rhyme lyrics – is ultimately unable to cope with the pent-up bitterness and musical aspirations of the young." They had "almost single-handedly given pop a musical authority which only the deaf cannot acknowledge and only the ignorant cannot hear".

Bassist and singer Jack Bruce talked so positively about Cream's working methods that viewers might have wondered why they had called it a day: "The songs that we play are really unimportant: they're just like jumping-off points for improvisation, and the only things that are set are the beginnings and endings of most of our things. In between, which can go on for ever, is just improvised, and we never know who's going to take the lead and what's going to happen next: it just happens depending on the atmosphere and the way we feel."

Paul and George both watched the documentary (Ringo watched snatches, but was also channel-hopping to *Rowan & Martin's Laugh-In* on BBC2), and Jack Bruce's delight in Cream's musical freedom should have given them pause for thought. Here was a band with a strong musical rapport, which had nevertheless decided to split up. The Beatles, in the meantime, were plodding on despite an obvious lack of rapport of any kind.

On Monday, January 6, any hope that The Beatles might have emerged refreshed from the weekend dissipated quickly. Harrison arrived late, having suffered from insomnia during the night, and tried to interest his bandmates, unsuccessfully, with 'Hear Me Lord'. Other new material was attempted, including 'Two Of Us', 'Carry That Weight' and Starr's 'Octopus's Garden' (the last two of which would eventually appear on their 1969 album, *Abbey Road*). They thrashed away at 'Don't Let Me Down', tinkering with its rhythm and its lyrics without creating any noticeable improvement. They talked, jammed and noodled aimlessly, and lurched into a series of old songs, including 'Dizzy Miss Lizzy',

'Money (That's What I Want)' and even George Formby's 'Leaning On A Lamp-Post'.

More constructively, they spent some time actively seeking venue ideas for their anticipated live concert. They downed instruments around midday and went out on a scouting mission; however, they returned to the studio shortly afterwards with nothing decided. "I remember going to scout locations around Twickenham," says Michael Lindsay-Hogg. "I don't know whose idea that was, but if you take it that George and Ringo were slightly less enthusiastic about the idea of Tunisia, it might have been George who said, 'If we're going to do this, why don't we get in the car and find somewhere to do it around here?' A few of us got in a car and drove around, but it was a particularly unpromising place to play a big rock'n'roll concert."

Denis O'Dell, head of Apple Films, had suggested another amphitheatre, this time in Tripoli, Libya, where he had enjoyed a performance by an Italian opera company years before. "Denis was around because he'd worked on a couple of their earlier movies," says Michael, "and he would toss bits of meat into the cage, which were always tasty but not always practical, because he wasn't there on a day-to-day basis. He'd chat a bit and then go off again. I think the amphitheatre that we'd all talked about was the one in Tunisia, not Libya."

The Beatles discussed how inspiring the feedback from an audience would be, but George, remembering their previous concerts, was concerned that the audience might consist only of screaming young female Beatlemaniacs. Yoko Ono chipped in with a highly conceptual idea: that The Beatles perform to 20,000 empty seats, which would represent "the invisible, nameless everybody in the world". Paul ran briefly with Yoko's idea, suggesting that they play one concert to a real audience, and another to empty seats.

Their efforts to decide on a concert venue seemed to be going the same way as the rehearsals. Just as they would switch capriciously from one song to another, lacking the discipline to stick to their new numbers and work constructively on them, so they would also hop from one concert idea to another, never considering any of them in any depth before moving on.

And just as there were moments of tomfoolery during the music rehearsals, jokes would occasionally be thrown into conversations about possible gigs. That afternoon, Ringo suggested they play on a riverboat, as they did on the Mersey back in the early days. Paul raised the possibility of The Beatles playing in the nude, to which George added that it might be better if the audience were naked rather than the performers. When they returned to the subject later that day, Paul was advocating building an artificial set resembling the Colosseum in Rome, and having The Beatles come in together with some real, live lions.

"Ideas were flying round at a terrific rate in those days," recalls Michael Lindsay-Hogg, "and they had all these ambitions and things they wanted to do. But at the same time, they were like people who'd been married a long time but didn't want to stay together. There was a lot of activity in the air, and because they were The Beatles, like a kind of musical royalty, the big ideas seemed possible."

The most infamous scene on that Monday – and it was a scene – occurred in a long discussion during a rehearsal of 'Two Of Us', when Paul was talking about the musical suggestions he was making to other members of the band. The scene is there for all to see in the *Let It Be* film. Perhaps unwisely, Paul brought up the 1968 'Hey Jude' recording sessions to illustrate his point, recalling how he had vetoed a lead-guitar part that George had initially wanted to play between vocal phrases.

"I always hear myself annoying you," Paul told George. "Look, I'm not trying to *get* you. I'm just saying, 'Look, lads – the band – shall we do it like this?'"

"Look," replied George, "I'll play whatever you want me to play, or I won't play *at all* if you don't want me to play. Whatever it takes to please you, I'll do it."

George was evidently having more fun with his side project, the Apple musical he was writing with Derek Taylor. The Beatles' press officer had officially announced the project to the media that day, and he and George were said to be working on it in the evenings at Apple and at Kinfauns. The main stage setting for the drama would be a recreation of Derek's press office on the third storey of 3 Savile Row, with his desk as the centrepiece. *The Beatles Book Monthly* reported: "Since his office is reputed to have in it some of the prettiest and most mini-skirted (should that be LEAST?) birds in London, the setting sounds just right for a good-looking good-sounding musical!"

As Tuesday dawned and The Beatles awoke and readied themselves for another gruelling day in Twickenham, an impressive assortment of other VIPs prepared to assemble at Marlborough House, the grand brick mansion on the Mall in London. This was the Commonwealth Prime Ministers' Conference, involving the heads of state of 24 nations. Over the course of the next week, British premier Harold Wilson would rub shoulders with leaders such as Indira Gandhi of India, Pierre Trudeau of Canada and Archbishop Makarios of Cyprus and discuss international issues of the day. Topics debated inside the conference chamber included the problem of Rhodesia – whose majority black population were governed by Ian Smith's government of exclusively white ministers – and immigration from Commonwealth countries into Britain. One subject that came up in various meetings outside the chamber was the Biafran crisis.

Enormous numbers of people were dying in this bitter conflict in West Africa. According to the Red Cross, at one point between 8,000 and 10,000 people were starving to death every day as a result of the Nigerian Civil War. In 1967, following a series of clashes between the different peoples of Nigeria, the eastern region had seceded from the country, forming the independent state of Biafra. The Nigerian government sent troops to recapture the territory, which was particularly rich in oil. Fighting continued for many months, and the Nigerian Navy enforced a blockade, preventing Biafra from receiving food, medical supplies and weapons. The word Biafra was now synonymous with shocking images of starving children, and the subject would enter The Beatles' conversation that day.

That morning at Twickenham found Paul back on the piano, trying out some new songs: 'The Long And Winding Road', which lacked a complete lyric at that stage; 'Golden Slumbers', a lullaby; and 'Carry That Weight', which seemed to anticipate the legacy the group would always bear. The last two songs would eventually appear on *Abbey Road*, and it's interesting that on that Tuesday, Paul played 'Carry That Weight' immediately after 'Golden Slumbers', prefiguring the medley construction of the closing section of that album. Paul had been playing other pieces during the sessions that were also destined to become *Abbey Road* tracks: 'Maxwell's Silver Hammer', 'Oh! Darling' and 'She Came In Through The Bathroom Window'.

The elusive new "rocker" The Beatles had been craving had its genesis on that Tuesday. Paul was periodically tinkering with a pounding bass riff, and he started tentatively singing some words over it. These were the sketchy beginnings of 'Get Back', which would eventually have the honour of being the final live song played in public by all four Beatles.

The idea of playing live to the public again featured prominently in their discussions that day. Paul was keen that they should play a live show, but, cognisant that his bandmates, especially George, were less enthusiastic about the plan, he decided to address one of their potential concerns: what if they played a gig and it went badly? What if their performance was under par, for example? Paul's solution was simple: if the footage isn't up to scratch, he said, they could simply discard it.

On this fourth day of rehearsals, Paul could no longer contain his frustrations at the lack of collective drive behind the new project. He even dared to diagnose the malaise within the group. "We've been very negative since Mr Epstein passed away," he pointed out. "We haven't been positive. That's why all of us in turn have been sick of the group, you know: there's nothing positive in it; it is a bit of a drag. It's like when you're growing up and then your daddy goes away at a certain point, and then you stand on your own feet. Daddy has gone away now, you know…" The cure, he decided, was a bit of old-fashioned discipline – a commodity that had been lacking since their manager's death in 1967. But this time it was down to the group themselves to apply the discipline from within. "Mr Epstein, he said, sort of, 'Get suits on,' and we did. And so we were always fighting that discipline a bit. But now it's silly to fight that discipline if it's our own. It's self-imposed these days, so we do as little as possible. But I think we need a bit more if we're going to get on with it."

George was griping that day about the whole idea of a live concert, arguing that he would prefer that they recorded their new batch of songs in a studio, as they usually did. That way, they could work carefully on the recordings, perfecting them until they were happy with the results. If they played the songs live, he said, they would "come out like a compromise". George's attitude cut right across the grain of the project, which was supposed to be a departure from the old studio complexity and a return to unadorned live ensemble playing.

Paul strongly disagreed that the songs would be a compromise: his argument was that they were still a fine band and could do an excellent job: "I really think we're very good. And we can get it together if we think that we want to do these songs – great, we can just do it great, you know."

Michael Lindsay-Hogg didn't approve of the idea that they play a concert here in Twickenham: not only was it a cop-out and far less cinematically exciting than, say, a performance in an African amphitheatre, but also they were *The Beatles* and should be setting their sights higher. "Well, one of the things that's wrong about doing the show here is that it's too easy," he said. Recalling their recent scouting expedition, he continued: "Like when we are in the car, looking for locations and glorified boutiques, I think that's wrong. But just doing it in the backyard – I mean, it's literal: it's almost your backyard, Twickenham – there's no balls to the show at all. I mean, there's no balls in any of us, I'm included, and that's why I think we are being soft about it. You are The Beatles, you aren't four jerks; you know what I mean."

The problem, Paul then pointed out, was that they didn't want to go abroad (meaning that one or two members of the group had vetoed that idea). George confirmed that he didn't view the prospect of an overseas gig as an exciting adventure. "You know it's going to be the same thing as here," he said. "It's going to be a bit nicer place to be in, but it's going to be even more complicated trying to plug in on all the mikes and tapes and all that crap."

Michael returned to his vision for the big concert, in an attempt to enthuse the performers in his production. "Think of the helicopter shot over the amphitheatre, with the water, with the lights," he urged, reminding them that it would be lit by torches and attended by "2,000 Arabs… Visually, it's fantastic."

As the director's words once again fell on stony ground, Paul started thinking aloud about how they might bring something new, a gimmick of some kind, to the concert. He recalled a show they had played years before in Wimbledon, which had been different not only because it was put on just for their fan club, but also because they played "in a cage". The show he was talking about had taken place at the Wimbledon Palais on December 14, 1963. Fearing that their stage might be damaged by rabid Beatlemaniacs, the management of the Palais had erected a metal barrier to keep the audience back.

It was at this point during the sessions, three weeks and two days before they took the West End of London by surprise, that Paul tabled the proposition of playing an illicit or "naughty" concert. One location that came to his mind was at the heart of the British Establishment: the Houses of Parliament in London. "Could you get it for us," he asked Michael, "the Houses of Parliament?" He continued: "We should do the show in a place where we're not allowed to do it. Like, we should *trespass*. Go in, set up, and get moved, and that should be the show. Get forcibly ejected... still trying to play your numbers and the police lifting you... you have to take a bit of violence."

"I think that's too dangerous," countered Michael. "I mean, that's an interesting thought if you're going to get beaten up." Perhaps imagining the medical treatment the group might need after being roughed up, the director then made another concert-venue suggestion: what about playing in a hospital? The idea was ignored for the time being, but may have registered with Paul, who would explore the idea minutes later.

In the meantime, John picked up on Paul's forbidden-venue idea with two possible locations, evidently not serious. One was Manila, capital of the Philippines, where The Beatles had been treated roughly in July 1966 after they unwittingly made a diplomatic faux pas by failing to attend a lunch in their honour hosted by Imelda Marcos, wife of the president. The other was Memphis, Tennessee.

They had played Memphis in August 1966 during their final tour of the USA, and had found the atmosphere tense and nasty. Devout Christians in many states were furious about John's notorious comparison of The Beatles to Jesus Christ. During a conversation earlier in the year with his friend Maureen Cleave, a British journalist, he had casually predicted: "Christianity will go. It will vanish and shrink. I needn't argue about that; I'm right and I'll be proved right. We're more popular than Jesus now." The interview had been published without a fuss in the *London Evening Standard* in March but after it was reprinted in the US teenage magazine *Datebook* that August, the protests, threats and record-burnings began.

Memphis is such a God-fearing place, there is said to be "a church on every corner". Robed Ku Klux Klan members patrolled outside the city's Mid-South Coliseum, where The Beatles were booked to perform. And at an early point in the evening show, as they played George's 'If I Needed Someone', somebody threw a firecracker on stage, which exploded. As their press officer Tony Barrow recalled, "... everybody, all of us at the side of the stage, including the three Beatles on stage, all looked immediately at John Lennon. We would not at that moment have been surprised to see that guy go down."

Liverpool Metropolitan Cathedral came up as a suggestion at this point as well – probably from Ringo, whose thinking seemed to be rooted in the city of his birth. Construction of this striking conical building had only been completed two years before, and a rock concert would surely have outraged the city's many Catholics. Paul then mentioned an orphanage, and George went into a light-hearted reverie about playing song requests, with each number played in honour of a specific person: "Each song is aimed at somebody – 'This one is for Enoch Powell.' 'I'd like to dedicate this one to Harold Wilson, the Singing Nun*, and General Washington. It's called…'" At which point John appended a typically comical title, presumably picturing Britain's aforementioned tobacco-puffing prime minister: "Up Yer Pipe."

Michael turned to the joker to see if he could extract some more sensible opinions from him. Where did John think they ought to play? "I'm warming up to the idea of an asylum," he replied.

Undeterred, Paul began thinking out loud about a performance that would be more than a concert; an ambitious event that would have a strong altruistic element to it. "We should send planes to Biafra and rescue all the people, and then play at the airport as they come in. Do a show for them – Biafrans."

Only a year and a half later, after The Beatles had disbanded, George Harrison would organise just such an event that combined music with internationalist compassion, *The Concert For Bangladesh*, whose mission was to raise money to help people affected by floods on the Asian subcontinent. But on this winter's day in Twickenham, he wasn't noticeably inspired by his bandmate's grandiose but well-meaning proposal to improve the lives of thousands of starving Africans. "Don't they say charity begins at home?" he remarked.

"So we will do it at George's house," Paul fired back.

"Let's do the show right here," said Ringo, echoing the old movie cliché.

Picking up from his Biafran suggestion, Paul continued: "Say we were doing it in an airport: you could stop the people from coming and going. They've all got planes to catch; like, you get a lot of people all the time going for planes and looking. It would be

---

* The Singing Nun was a holy woman from Belgium, a member of the Catholic Dominican Order who had enjoyed a huge hit with the infectious song 'Dominique' in the early sixties.

a *scene*. Or in a hospital: they can't get up – except at the finale, when John walks over to the little girl and says, 'Come, ye,' and she gets up and walks."

Paul was edging into biblical territory here, daring to suggest that the group – and John in particular – replicate one of the Miracles of Jesus, as when the Son of God raised Lazarus from the dead. Though this is likely to have been tongue-in-cheek, a casual jest to keep the desperately needed ideas for a live show rolling along, there were echoes here of John's troublesome "Jesus" remark.

Later, after they tinkered with a few half-hearted numbers, Paul addressed his frustrations with the attitudes of his old friends. "I don't see why any of you, if you're not interested, got yourselves into this," he said. "What's it for? It can't be for the money. Why are you here? I'm here because I want to do a show, but I really don't feel a lot of support."

Paul went on to deliver a petulant ultimatum. "There's only two choices," he said. "We're going to do it or we're not going to do it. And I want a decision. Because I'm not interested in spending my fucking days farting around here while everyone makes up their minds whether they want to do it or not. If everyone else wants to do it, great, but I don't have to be here." If the experience of this project ended up like that of the White Album, he said, maybe it should be their last venture together. "There's no point in hanging on."

Overhearing some of these intense discussions was Paul Bond, the clapper boy of the three-man camera team filming the rehearsals. "There's no question that there were these rows going on all the while, particularly between Paul and John. John really didn't want to have anything to do with it all: he was ready to be off. And I remember one conversation, when Paul said something like, 'Listen, we're going to split up, we've all had enough of it.'

He had as well. 'But we've got this contract. Let's just finish this film and this album, let's just get it done and then we can all fuck off.' Which was quite a sensible way of looking at it, I thought.''

One of the difficulties that rankled with Paul McCartney at the time was John's persistent reticence. The former leader of The Beatles was now contributing very little to their discussions and allowing decisions to be made around him. The reasons for this acute passivity were tightly interlinked. Partly to blame were the deteriorating relationships between the four band members; another reason was John's still-burgeoning, intimate and obsessive relationship with Yoko Ono; and yet another was the couple's addiction to heroin.

As the days trudged on, it was becoming painfully obvious that John's songwriting was at a low ebb. On Wednesday, January 8, Paul confronted him directly about his lack of new material. "Have you written anything?" he asked as the spools of an audio-recorder turned nearby. He sounded like a schoolteacher berating a child for failing to do his homework.

"No," replied John.

"We're going to be faced with a crisis, you know."

"When I'm up against the wall, Paul, you'll find me at my best."

Paul didn't sound convinced. "Yeah, I know... but I just wish you'd come up with the goods."

"Look, I think I've got Sunday off."

"Yeah? Well, I hope you can deliver."

"I'm hoping for a little rock'n'roller... 'Sammy With His Mammy'."

Whether Paul picked it up or not, John's midweek suggestion that he may have time to write songs during the forthcoming weekend surely carried within it a hint of frustration and protest. Here they were every day, spending the daylight hours struggling with a handful of new songs and finding the slightest excuse to grind out cover versions of old favourites. A clear subtext of John's statement was: if he could only have some time off on his own (or with Yoko), he could come back with perhaps two or three great new songs for the project. As it happened, John wouldn't even have that Sunday free: much of it would be occupied with unexpected Beatles business.

In interviews after The Beatles' break-up, John claimed that songwriting had usually been a trial for him. In 1980, three days before he died, he told an interviewer that when he had looked over previous interviews, he realised "that I'm always complaining about how hard it is to write, or how much I suffer when I'm writing – that almost every song I've ever written has been absolute torture... I always think there's nothing there, it's shit, it's no good, it's not coming out, this is garbage... and even if it does come out, I think, 'What the hell is it anyway?'"

In the same interview, he claimed that he only had a week to write songs for *Sgt. Pepper*. It is surely no coincidence that his songs on that record, more than those on any other Beatles album, highlight the way he used "found materials" as starting-points for his songs. 'Being For The Benefit Of Mr. Kite' has snatches of lyric lifted from a Victorian circus poster he found in a Sevenoaks antique shop, while his section of 'A Day In The Life' refers to a 1967 *Daily Mail* report on the preponderance of potholes in the roads of Blackburn, Lancashire, and 'Lucy In The Sky With Diamonds', despite that glaring LSD abbreviation, was prompted by a painting his son Julian brought home from school. If he wasn't using found materials as inspiration, he was triggered by snatches of conversation, as when a discussion with the actor Peter Fonda during an LSD trip in 1965 sparked the lyric of 'She Said She Said'.

But there was little to ignite his creativity during those grey winter's days in Twickenham, apart from his relationship with Yoko Ono. This had clearly inspired one of the songs he had brought to the table, 'Don't Let Me Down', which was given one decent full-band run-through that Wednesday. At the end of that performance, John gave one of his comical mock stage announcements. "God bless you, ladies and gentlemen," he slurred. "I'd just like to say a sincere farewell from Rocky and The Rollers. This is Dirty Mac himself sayin'…" He was cut off as Paul suggested they have another crack at 'I've Got A Feeling'. Dirty Mac had been the name of the supergroup featuring John and Yoko in *The Rolling Stones Rock And Roll Circus*.

One of the bands they had worked with on that production was The Who. And at the same time that The Beatles were slogging through oldies and scraps of new music at Twickenham, Pete Townshend and his bandmates were hitting new heights of creativity at IBC Studios in London's Portland Place, where they were recording their fourth album, *Tommy*. All four members were pulling together to realise their leader's lofty vision of a "rock opera" about the spiritual journey of the deaf, dumb and blind boy of the title. While The Beatles were insisting on going back to basics sonically, The Who were arranging and overdubbing furiously, Townshend playing keyboards as well as electric and acoustic guitar, and John Entwistle adding French horn, trumpet and flugelhorn as well as bass guitar, while their drummer Keith Moon was an orchestra unto himself, joyfully whacking timpani and a gong as well as a drum kit that boasted two bass drums. The finished oeuvre would include the unforgettable songs 'Pinball Wizard', 'I'm Free' and 'See Me, Feel Me' and take The Who into the realms of complex progressive rock: it even dared to begin with an 'Overture', and there was an 'Underture' for good measure too.

The Moody Blues were also scheduled to record in a few days' time. The former rhythm-and-blues outfit from the West Midlands would enter Decca Studios in West Hampstead to embark on their third concept album in succession. *On The Threshold Of A Dream* would use spacey sound effects, poetry and instruments such as cello, flute, piccolo, oboe, harmonica and Mellotron in addition to the standard set-up of vocals, guitar, bass and drums to explore the world of dreams.

As The Beatles ground away on the soulless soundstage, they were still, as far as they were vaguely aware and as the film-makers and the group's entourage believed, working towards a spectacular final concert. The date of Saturday, January 18, had been mooted, but was apparently giving way now to Monday, January 20. The only problem was, nobody had a clue where in the world they would be playing. Michael Lindsay-Hogg's Tunisian amphitheatre idea was still the favoured option, and Denis O'Dell's rival Libyan amphitheatre proposal was floating around. Ethiopia was also mentioned. One day, Mal Evans told Kevin Harrington that the whole team would be going to Greece to film The Beatles' live performances, but the next day Mal said those plans had been cancelled. "They talked about playing in the Grand Canyon as well," says Chris O'Dell. "Coming from Arizona, I thought that would be cool."

Ringo suggested the British Overseas Territory of Gibraltar, at the southern end of Spain, bringing the possibilities a little closer to home once again. Also mentioned in the film studio later that Wednesday was Tahiti (where The Beatles had holidayed as a respite from Beatlemania back in 1964), though that may have been simply because its name alliterated with those two other mooted exotic locations, Tunisia and Tripoli.

George complained that transporting all the equipment and the people to Tunisia was an "impractical" scheme, and Paul countered with an ambitious but reasonably practical idea: that the tickets for the show include transportation by sea for the spectators, by way of "a couple of boats, like the *QE2*". That way, he enthused, the exotic overseas performance could become a reality. "Right! We get a nice time and a bit of sun." This succeeded in perking up John, who reminisced about those blissful days in Rishikesh less than a year ago, when they sat on the roofs of the cottages where they were staying, singing and playing in the sunshine.

"Paul's idea was that they'd rehearse on the boat," says Michael, "and that we would bring some of our audience with us. Although we would pick people up in Tunisia, we would bring an English contingent on the boat with us, which would sail from Liverpool to Tunisia, and of course then film the boat and the rehearsals on the boat. This is when the whole idea expanded to very extravagant proportions. But only The Beatles would've been capable of executing such a thing, because they had the money to do it – although it was quickly running out – if that's what they wanted to do. They could probably have got it paid for by a television company anyway.

"John was for it – I think back then, John was for anything that would get him out of the film studio and get him away from sitting with the other three. I think he'd already partly decided that he and Yoko would embark on a different artistic career. He was quite happy to be anywhere as long as he and Yoko were together, and he was happy to play the music and liked the idea of the amphitheatre. And Paul was for it, and I think Ringo thought there was something to it. But George was in a different position, really: I think he had gotten very fed up with touring after the 1966 tour, and he really just wanted to make an album. He didn't want there to be a TV special, he didn't want to be filmed, particularly; he wanted to work on the music.

"If it sounds like George was a negative person, he wasn't at all. In fact, he was very sweet, extremely affable, very interested in what you were thinking as well as what he was thinking; he was funny. But he definitely had opinions about what was right for them to do and for him to do, and by this time he was also feeling much more confident in stating those opinions. Originally he'd been the young one. Neil Aspinall told me the story that before they were The Beatles, John and Paul would walk along the street discussing their great ideas and George would be behind them, carrying the guitar cases. I actually liked George very much and found him very *un*-negative. But he was stubborn."

George dismissed the idea of using a boat, calling it "very expensive and insane". It would have to be a "bloody big boat", he said, laughing, "bigger than the *Royal Iris*!" The *Royal Iris* was a 159-foot-long Art Deco-style ferry that had hosted dance cruises known as "Riverboat Shuffles" on the River Mersey, and The Beatles had played on it four times between August 1961 and September 1962.

John suggested they use "Aristotle's yacht", by which he meant the *Christina O*, a superyacht owned by the shipping tycoon Aristotle Onassis, who had married Jackie Kennedy back in October. This was a 325-foot-long vessel that had been built in 1943 for the Canadian Navy, which had been lavishly refitted in the fifties and had hosted parties attended by such luminaries as Winston Churchill, Elizabeth Taylor and Marilyn Monroe.

Despite George's quibbles, the El Djem amphitheatre idea became the favoured option, and Michael Lindsay-Hogg recalls that it looked like it would really happen. "We got to the stage where we were all going to go to Tunisia. They'd already bought airline tickets for Mal and Neil to fly out there, to check the security issues in the hotels and stuff, do a recce." Monday, January 13, was the date when Mal and Neil would be flying to Africa.

"They were all talking about doing this concert," says the technical engineer Dave Harries, "and I remember phoning people and trying to find a standby generator that could be shipped at very short notice out to somewhere."

Unsurprisingly, there seems to have been some confusion within The Beatles' entourage between the two amphitheatres discussed – the one in Tunisia and the other in Tripoli. Mal Evans mentioned Tripoli rather than Tunisia in a 'Mal's Diary' piece for *The Beatles Book Monthly*. Also, plans were mentioned for food to be transported to the site of the concerts from the same suppliers who helped to stock a nearby American air base. By far the most likely contender here is the Wheelus Air Base, a large facility on the coast of Tripoli that the Americans were still using in early 1969.

The Beatles entered into a surreal discussion about adopting individual code names for their overseas voyage, such as the American Secret Service used for the president and other VIPs in radio and telephone messages. The current outgoing US president, Lyndon B. Johnson, was addressed by American spooks as "Volunteer", and the president-elect, Richard Nixon, was "Searchlight".

The Beatles' cyphers were the names of foreign countries – George was France and Ringo was Russia, for example – which caused some brief hilarity in the film studio. When Ringo's code name was mentioned, John thought they were actually talking about playing in Russia, and there was similar confusion when George was addressed as France.

"I think the code-name idea would have come from Paul rather than anyone else," says Michael. "Sometimes there'd be an idea, and because their brains were those of musicians, they would riff on the idea as if it were a melody. So if the melody was 'We're all going to Tunisia,' then one of them would say, 'Hey, we should have code names so no one knows who we are,' and then they'd go further into the thing and Paul or John would say, 'George should be

France, and Ritchie, you should be Russia, and I'll be Scandinavia' or whatever. That would've been more of a riff than a serious idea."

George may have taken to his code name more than the other three, because there are several photographs of him taken in the seventies, after The Beatles' break-up, in which he is wearing a dark T-shirt with the word FRANCE emblazoned across it in white capital letters.

Before they parted company that Wednesday in January, John reached his peak of enthusiasm for a foreign show, making a clear case to the others for "getting away from it all" for the conclusion of the project: "Every time we've done an album at EMI, we ask, 'Why are we stuck in here? We could be in LA, or in France!' And every time we do it, and here we are again building a bloody castle around us." A different location, he argued, would immediately remove the problem of deciding what "the gimmick" would be this time. "*God's* the gimmick," he said, fantasising that they could time their performance to coincide with a beautiful sunrise.

On the next day, Thursday, Linda Eastman accompanied Paul into the studio. George arrived late, after 11 a.m., saying: "I was so hungry today, I had to be late just to eat my breakfast… if you want an excuse." There were some discussions about playing the big show at Twickenham, and Paul was keen on making the rehearsals more realistic, to reflect where they would be standing and the positions of the amplifiers during the show. "Bass amps in the middle, do you think, and guitar on the side?" he asked. "It's a bit silly rehearsing sitting, facing this way, when we're actually going to play standing, facing *that* way. We should get into that."

This sensible idea wasn't taken up by the other Beatles, and George filled the silence with a joke. "We've still got our dance steps to learn yet," he quipped.

"Oh yeah… and the jokes in between the numbers," replied Paul.

For the past six days they had been spending arguably too much time playing scrappy cover versions – songs by Elvis Presley, Gene Vincent, Smokey Robinson and even George Formby. But when George Harrison asked if they should play "other people's tunes as well" during the live show, it was as if the idea had never crossed their minds.

"I don't know any," claimed John.

"I don't like anybody else's," alleged Paul.

Speaking apparently to George, John said: "I can only just bear doing *your* songs, never mind strangers'."

Here was another put-down for George, who was obviously blossoming as a songwriter but had been struggling to get John and Paul to rehearse some of his latest compositions during the sessions, even the sublime 'All Things Must Pass', which would become the title track of his chart-busting 1970 solo triple album. George recalled years later: "The problem was that John and Paul had written songs for so long that it was difficult. First of all, because they had such a lot of tunes, they automatically thought that theirs should be the priority. So, for me, I'd always have to wait through 10 of their songs before they would even listen to one of mine. That's why *All Things Must Pass* had so many songs, because it was like, you know, I had been constipated."

As the group rehearsed on that Thursday in Twickenham, an exotic foreign show wasn't off the cards altogether, and there was some talk about the sound equipment they might use on a boat. But most of the working day was devoted to some serious – and not-so-serious – playing.

The Commonwealth conference was still in progress and in the news, and the topic of immigration was being kicked around again by politicians, the media and the British public. Right-wingers were arguing for an enforced repatriation of immigrants from the Commonwealth, hauling out the specious arguments that Britain was "too crowded" and was being "swamped" by all these conspicuously non-white people from India and Pakistan.

It was at this point that 'Get Back' began to develop as a song. As he often did when working up a composition, Paul sang snatches of gibberish while they played; some of the words and phrases that emerged would be discarded and some would remain in the finished number. He riffed about Pakistanis, Arizona, California grass, Puerto Ricans and Mohicans, and introduced two characters, Joe and Theresa. Paul sang about somebody with an uncertain sexual identity, who thought she was a woman but was really "another man", and other lines were present that are now preserved in the finished song. The chorus was now fixed as "Get back to where you once belonged".

Paul laughed and commented on the lack of meaning in the lyrics, though he was only following the long-established Beatles tradition of writing vaguely plausible words that scanned with the music. George commented that it wouldn't matter if he used any "rubbish" for the text of the song, as The Band had done on their track 'Caledonia Mission', with its watchman, garden gate, magistrate and hexagram. But for a while, one of the lyrical themes of 'Get Back' would be a satire on racist attitudes to immigration.

Sticking to the lyrical theme of 'Get Back', Paul began to improvise another song about Enoch Powell and his arguments for repatriation. The lyric had Powell telling immigrants to "get back to your Commonwealth homes", and Ted Heath (leader of the Opposition, who had sacked Powell from the Shadow Cabinet the previous April) telling Powell: "Enoch, you'd better go home." Harold Wilson came into the song at this point, saying something barely intelligible. The song's chorus was simply the word

"Commonwealth" called out by Paul, who was audibly amused when John responded with the word "Yes?" in a high voice with a distinctly proletarian accent – a quick-witted interpretation of the word "common". Paul continued the number by name-checking various Commonwealth countries, including Pakistan, India, Australia and New Zealand, though one decidedly non-Commonwealth destination stood out: Tucson, a populous city in southern Arizona.

The Beatles played 'I've Got A Feeling' again that day, spending a disproportionate amount of time rehearsing the end of the bridge, with its slowly descending bluesy guitar notes, to Paul's strict specifications. It was clear that the lyrics of John's section were still fluid: in addition to seeing the sunshine and pulling their socks up, people were still having "a facelift". Paul was also sketching out the words to 'Let It Be' that day, and name-checked a British music paper as he threw in random lines for a solo piano performance of the number, singing "Read the *Record Mirror*, let it be."

The weather outside was dangerously changeable. That day, more than 100 vehicles were involved in pile-ups on the M1 and M10 motorways in Hertfordshire. Police complained that despite widespread warnings of hazardous freezing fog over England and Wales, motorists had continued to drive at high speeds, risking the safety of themselves and other road users. Sixty-three people were now in hospital as a result.

It was still chilly on the next day, Friday, January 10, but the weather was mainly dry, with periods of sunshine. For The Beatles, this was the day when everything would change. Before it did, they played some more music and engaged in some jolly banter. That morning their music publisher, Dick James, visited the studios and he, Paul and Michael Lindsay-Hogg had a relaxed conversation that took in the previous night's television and the table manners of young children. Paul was chuckling about Thursday's edition of *The Eamonn Andrews Show*, a popular late-night chat programme, which featured the much-married actress Zsa Zsa Gabor and the satirist Peter Cook. When the presenter Eamonn Andrews asked his other guests for their opinions on Gabor, Cook replied – in front of her – that he thought she was a vain, untalented non-event.

Later, Paul asked Ringo if Neil Aspinall had called him the evening before. Ringo said no, and Paul explained that the call had been about some "news on the wheeling-and-dealing scene". It became apparent what he meant when George, John and Yoko arrived. George revealed that he had also received a call from Neil, who had been asking for a meeting with the group on Saturday. John, who said he hadn't had a call, quibbled about the weekend timing. "Only because we're busy every other day," explained George.

"What about evenings, you know, about seven or eight or something?" asked John.

"But he was very excited," said George.

"Was he? Good news?"

"Yes."

"Oh, I'll come for good news, you know. I don't want to have any troubles," said John as, several yards away, Paul ran through his pretty piano accompaniment for 'The Long And Winding Road'.

"It's so good... He just told me briefly what it was. But I'll just have to whisper it or write it on a bit of paper and you'll have to swallow it," joked George.

"Is it anything to do with Pig over there?" asked John, referring rudely to Dick James.

The news wasn't to do with their publisher, though: it was that John Eastman had come over to London. The American lawyer, brother of Linda Eastman, was one of the potential saviours of the

Apple business – although Allen Klein was still lurking in the shadows as well.

Michael Lindsay-Hogg says that The Beatles opened up about their financial problems during their downtime at Twickenham. "I remember having lunch breaks up in the restaurant. Usually it would be the four of them, plus Yoko, plus me, and we were occasionally joined by lighting cameraman Tony Richmond, and sometimes people who came down, like Peter Brown, so we'd all sit and chat. And that's when they started to talk, which I was fascinated by, about them being on their way to being broke. So much money had come in, but a lot of it had been spent on their philanthropic interests. Also, I think Brian Epstein had made deals that couldn't be collected on. There were foreign royalties owing, and they weren't really getting that much per album with the original deal. So they were worried about running out of money. That didn't mean that they didn't have their Rolls-Royces and their Mercedes or whatever, and it didn't mean that they couldn't plan to take a boat to Tunisia," he laughs, "but they were concerned that much more was going out than was coming in.

"I remember being in the control room one day during the sessions, and hearing John say to the others that he'd met this guy quite recently who was an American who looked after the Stones, and he thought it might be the guy to help them with their financial problems, and his name was Allen Klein. I also think that he was in George's orbit, suggesting that he maybe could have a solo career as well as being one of The Beatles. He later organised *The Concert For Bangladesh* for George. And I think Allen was, partly through John and partly through George, finding his way to get to The Beatles. Now, he could offer them a lot: he was a shrewd negotiator, he'd been in the business for a long time – he'd been Sam Cooke's manager. Some people didn't like Allen much, but I think he was very funny and very charming."

Dick James informed The Beatles that Vera Lynn would be on television on Saturday evening, on *The Rolf Harris Show*, singing her latest single: 'Good Night', a song from their White Album. The 51-year-old singer was fondly remembered as the Forces' Sweetheart who helped to raise British morale in World War Two with 'We'll Meet Again' and '(There'll Be Bluebirds Over) The White Cliffs of Dover'. Her cover of 'Good Night' turned the song into a waltz. "Sounds beautiful," said Dick.

John said he was under the impression that Vera had covered Paul's song 'The Fool On The Hill' from *Magical Mystery Tour*. Indeed she had, replied Dick: that was the B-side.

"So let's hope she gets a hit with that," said John.

There was already a cover of another White Album tune sitting at the top of the charts: 'Ob-La-Di, Ob-La-Da', performed by Marmalade. But Vera's new record didn't even tickle the Top 40, proving that covering a Beatles song didn't always guarantee instant chart success.

The musical that George had planned with Derek Taylor was apparently still a going concern: George mentioned it again that day. He also had a conversation with Michael about Magic Alex, the Greek wunderkind who was "busy building the recording studio" in the basement of the Apple building.

During the day's sessions The Beatles played a faster-than-usual version of 'Get Back', with John sharing lead vocals with Paul. Later, around lunchtime, George reportedly had an intense disagreement with John, which may have been the last straw, what with the ongoing misery of the Twickenham sessions and plans for a forthcoming live show that failed to enthuse him. It was subsequently alleged in the *Daily Sketch* that this wasn't just a verbal spat; that the two Beatles had a physical battle.

"Well, I think I'll be leaving… uh… leaving the band now," he announced to John.

"What?" replied his bandmate. "When?"

"Now," said George, adding some friendly advice: "Get a replacement. Or write in to the *NME* and get a few people."

George appeared briefly in the studios' small canteen, up a flight of stairs, where his bandmates and Mal Evans and Michael Lindsay-Hogg were having lunch. "See you round the clubs," he said.

George had a small piece of Apple business to complete before he walked out the door: he talked to Mal about paying some musicians that were booked to play on the 'King Of Fuh' record at Trident Studios. Various people, including Kevin Harrington and Dave Harries, watched as George put on his coat before he headed purposefully for the exit. "I remember George Harrison walked out, because he was fed up; I don't know why," says Dave Harries. "And I remember that George Martin had just backed across the car park in his Triumph Herald and knocked a dent in the door of George Harrison's Mercedes, and he didn't have time to tell him he'd dented his car before George walked out in a huff and drove off."

Paul walked into Denis O'Dell's production office and gave him the bad news. "That's it," he said. "We've split up. George has gone."

Mal Evans later wrote: "Of the four Paul was the most enthusiastic all along about doing the 'live' show. John would have gladly taken the whole production unit to Africa or America to find the right location. John and Ringo had mixed feelings about the plan, agreeing with Paul on a lot of the ideas but feeling this might not be the best way of making a 1969 Beatles TV film. George wasn't keen at all. Ever since the last Beatles tour of America in the summer of 1966 he has considered 'one night stands' to be a thing of the past, a backward step for a group he believes should concentrate on perfecting recordings rather than churning out the same programme of too-familiar songs on stages here and abroad.

"So on Friday at Twickenham George stated his case. Singing and playing together would always be fine with him and the last thing he was suggesting was any break-up of The Beatles. So that day, January 10, George didn't want to stay at Twickenham rehearsing for a show he couldn't believe in."

The Beatles could have packed up and gone home there and then, but they didn't: there was the faint hope that George would return, and there was also the possibility, as he had suggested, that they "get a replacement". John quickly suggested Eric Clapton, who was "just as good and not such a headache". In the meantime, Paul, Ringo, John and Yoko plodded on with the rehearsals, though the purpose of the exercise had now become even fuzzier than it had been before, if that were possible. The four of them launched into an aggressive jam – described by Michael as "half an hour of anger and frustration expressed with guitars and drums. Yoko sat on the edge of the rostrum on the blue cushion which had been George's and howled into his mike."

George drove back to Esher, where there was no Pattie to greet him at Kinfauns: she had gone to stay with friends, convinced that her husband and their glamorous French lodger Charlotte Martin were conducting an affair. George found Charlotte in the house alone and, possibly craving some kind of normality or continuity in his life, asked her to leave, then telephoned Pattie for a reconciliation. His surprisingly casual diary entry for that day, in red pen, reads: "got up went to Twickenham rehearsed until lunch time – left The Beatles – went home and in the evening did King of Fuh at Trident Studio". It also briefly documents his evening, which was spent visiting the home of his old friend Klaus Voorman and his wife Christine, where he "had chips". George and Pattie's marriage would survive for the time being, but whatever trust had existed between them seemed irreparably eroded.

That weekend, George got back into his car and back to his roots, driving more than 200 miles to see his parents at the bungalow he had bought for them in the village of Appleton, near Warrington. Travel would certainly have been an antidote to the stir-craziness of the Twickenham sessions, and his parents' house and garden were something of a refuge for him – the place where, not long ago, he had been inspired to write 'While My Guitar Gently Weeps'.

That Sunday, January 12, all four Beatles, plus Yoko and Linda, convened at Ringo's house to see if they could settle their differences. But there was more rancour and disagreement, and the meeting ended without resolution. On top of that, this was the Sunday that John had previously earmarked as a possible day for writing songs, after being challenged by Paul on his lack of new material. There was a consolation for George that day: the new Odeon multiplex cinema in London's Panton Street was showing on all four of its screens the film *Wonderwall*, whose soundtrack he had composed.

When the sessions continued the next morning at Twickenham, both George and John were absent. For much of the previous week, John had been noticeably taciturn. But that day, he gave an interview at Savile Row to the music journalist Ray Coleman in which he was extremely lucid and pessimistic about the difficulties at Apple. "I think it's a bit messy and it wants tightening up," he said. "We haven't got half the money people think we have. We have enough to live on, but we can't let Apple go on like this. We started off with loads of ideas of what we wanted to do, you know, an umbrella of different activities. But like one or two Beatles things, it didn't work out, because we weren't quick enough to realise that we needed a business brain to run the whole thing.

You can't offer facilities to poets and charities and film plans unless you have money coming in. It's been pie-in-the-sky from the start. Apple's losing money every week because it needs closely running by a businessman. We did it all wrong, you know, Paul and me running to New York, saying we'll do this and encourage this and that. It's got to be a business first – we realise that now. It needs a broom, and a lot of people there will have to go. It needs streamlining. It doesn't need to make vast profits, but if it carries on like this, all of us will be broke in the next six months."

Back at Twickenham, Neil Aspinall paid a visit to the studios and was surprised and concerned to find only half the group present. Paul was accompanied that day by Linda, and as the tape recorders rolled, they had a long conversation with Neil and Michael about John's relationship with Yoko, his current failure to communicate, and how this was affecting the group. They also talked about possible locations for the live show – again – and how it might be filmed, though nobody sounded fully convinced that it would really happen now. Paul said that because of the difficulties within the band everything was effectively on hold for the time being.

The Beatles were closer to splitting up, there and then, than they had ever been. Even Paul, who had been so gung-ho about the *Get Back* project, was being realistic and talking about a possible split.

Before they broke for lunch, they went to the studios' viewing theatre to see some rushes of the film they were supposed to be making. The mood improved slightly after John finally arrived at the studios mid-afternoon, and the three Beatles continued to develop 'Get Back', with Paul and John trying out surnames for the Loretta character in the lyrics – John suggesting "Loretta Marvin" at one stage – and Paul bringing in a mention of Tucson, Arizona, which he had already mentioned in their 'Commonwealth' jam. But they accomplished little else that day.

Around this point, Derek Taylor intervened, contacting George and persuading him that he had a responsibility to see the film project through to the end. "I felt that George's sense of decency could be touched," Derek recalled later. "And it was." George was apparently now in Liverpool, but planning to return.

For the time being the mood of uncertainty continued, and on the next day Michael wondered out loud if the cameras should be turned off. "We ought to figure out, shall we go on filming and playing," he said to Paul and John, "or do you want to rehearse or do you want to move into EMI and get out of this place and just do an album?"

"Well, the thing is," said Paul, "George is in Liverpool now and he's coming back tomorrow." He added that they should call a halt to filming, and the cameramen duly obliged.

There was still a great deal of confusion about what was and what wasn't happening. As far as some people on the project were aware, *Get Back* was all over. "I remember getting home one night after the day's shoot," says Paul Bond, "and the phone rang and it was the producer saying the boys had all split up and its all over, the job's off – 'We'll pay you to the end of the week, and thanks very much. Goodbye.' That was a terrible blow."

CHAPTER THREE

The Basement Tapes

George Harrison's departure from The Beatles – though it wasn't permanent, lasting less than a week – was a significant factor in the sequence of events that led up to the rooftop concert. If he had remained in the group, seen the Twickenham sessions through to the end, and been more favourably disposed towards plans to perform one or more concerts in a specially selected location, then the story of The Beatles in 1969 could have been very different.

It wouldn't necessarily have been better; there was always the prospect that the big concerts in Tunisia, Libya, the Grand Canyon, the Roundhouse, the Houses of Parliament or wherever would not have been entirely successful. For their last ever paying concert, at Candlestick Park in 1966, there were thousands of unsold tickets and empty seats, and the show was marred by the winds that often blew in from the nearby San Francisco Bay. As it was, The Beatles left us with a unique valedictory event – an unexpected "happening" that went down in history.

When George reunited with the rest of the group on Wednesday, January 15, he was in a strong position. The bond between him and his fellow Beatles was still solid; they had missed him and his playing, and he was an integral part of the group as far as their public image was concerned. The Beatles were and always would be John, Paul, George and Ringo. George was therefore able to lay down some conditions before he became a Beatle again.

During a meeting lasting several hours, he insisted that they jettison their plans for a live show in front of an audience, and that they decamp from Twickenham Studios to their own basement studio at Apple to make an album – to which the rest of the band agreed. The cameras would be rolling again, but this time they would be filming The Beatles making the record.

The idea of a climactic show wasn't completely dead: there was still the possibility that they would film an audience-free performance for the enjoyment of television viewers. But there would be no sunset show in the desert to a worshipful multi-ethnic crowd, no triumphant return to the Liverpool stage and no big event in a flour mill by the River Thames. Mal and Neil wouldn't be flying to Africa the next day to visit one of the likely amphitheatres, as they had originally planned.

Michael Lindsay-Hogg, for one, was disappointed. "We came close to doing the Tunisian trip. And I think we would've done it – perhaps not quite as ambitiously as taking the boat – if George hadn't said no. It would have been an extraordinary event if George hadn't put the kibosh on it."

Thousands of fans were crestfallen too. Three young women from North Shields penned a heartfelt "open letter" to *The Beatles Book Monthly*: "We have just heard that your long-awaited 'live' concert appearance has been scrapped for good. Just how much are faithful Beatle fans expected to take? We've stuck up for you through thick and thin, even though we haven't always agreed with you… We thought we were getting compensation for waiting so long for your third film, which still hasn't been started yet, but it appears that the waiting has to go on. Yes, we know we had 'Yellow Submarine' – and we all enjoyed it – but it wasn't you was it? Oh! we've had some great albums too, for which we are grateful, but we still yearned to see you live (if we were lucky enough to get tickets) and if not at least we would have seen you via our TV sets.

"We have been faithful followers now for 6½ years and intend to stay that way, to the lovable boys who revolutionised the pop-music world, who showed people that pop-artistes really *do* have talent and that long hair is not a sign of stupidity." The trio signed off with the peevish question: "Is this sudden disappointment a symbol of your gratitude??"

If the spirit of adventure had deserted The Beatles, it was present in spades on the other side of the Atlantic. On the same day that the group came to their new agreement, three Americans began their preparations for one of the greatest missions ever undertaken by humankind. Neil Armstrong, Edwin "Buzz" Aldrin and Michael Collins went into training for the Apollo 11 mission, the first manned landing on the moon. The three astronauts began a gruelling regimen of 14-hour working days that would continue for six months, right up to the day before the launch. They would go over the mission plans and work inside simulators for the various modules involved. Collins spent much of his time inside the Command and Service Module simulator, preparing him for his orbit of the moon while his colleagues did the more glamorous work down on its surface. Armstrong and Aldrin endured many hours in claustrophobic conditions in the Lunar Module simulator, rehearsing the historic landing they would make in July.

These being the days of the Space Race, the Russians were about to achieve a cosmic first before the Americans bagged the moon. January 15 was the day they launched Soyuz 5, and on the following day it would dock with its predecessor Soyuz 4 in orbit around the Earth. This would be the first time that humankind had docked any manned craft out there in space, and the first time that people had transferred from one craft to another in space. And they threw in a space walk for good measure.

Back on Earth, The Beatles were looking forward to using their new recording studio for the first time. This was the much-touted multi-track facility created for them by their house inventor, Magic Alex. George, who was particularly in awe of Alex's creations, took the engineer Glyn Johns to inspect the new studio. Glyn was horrified at what he saw. The recording console, he decided, "looked like something out of a 1930s Buck Rogers science fiction movie". There were several small speakers positioned around the walls – presumably one for each track of the recording system. When The Beatles gave it a try, the results were appalling.

Dave Harries remembers that he had to do some technical tinkering, using power amplifiers from EMI, before the desk was vaguely usable. "It was a shame, because it had some good ideas: instead of having swivelling needles for the sound levels on the tracks, it had oscilloscope metering, which you get on desks nowadays. But it was wired up wrongly and had the mains on it, which made it hum. The Beatles did a session on it, then listened to the results and walked out."

The whole studio was a technician's nightmare. Because it wasn't properly soundproofed, it was recording all kinds of noise in addition to the music they were trying to lay down. Sound was going into an old fireplace and reverberating up the chimney, and echoing behind some old oak doors. Apple staff could be heard walking across the ground floor above, and even fragments of their muffled conversations were going down on tape. The basement boiler that heated the building was now inside the studio, and the noises it made became part of the cacophony. It could be turned off, but in January that would have made for some chilly working conditions.

The Beatles quickly realised that if they were going to record here they needed some equipment that was up to the job, so George Martin arranged for some to be borrowed from EMI Studios in Abbey Road, including two four-track mixers. Dave Harries and another engineer, Keith Slaughter, collected the gear and painstakingly set it all up in the basement. They were assisted by a junior technician from EMI who was recruited in a hurry: Alan Parsons. "I couldn't believe it – there I was. One day I was making tea at Abbey Road, and the next day I was working with The Beatles at their studio."

Although The Beatles were inactive as a performing unit while they waited for their studio to be fixed, a flurry of press stories brought them back to the public's attention. Their sudden change of plans had caught *Melody Maker* on the hop: the paper went on sale on Thursday, January 16, with an outdated front-page story claiming that "A one-hour documentary film of the Beatles in the recording studios is currently being shot at London's Twickenham Studios, where The Beatles are rehearsing the songs for their projected live concerts." Derek Taylor was quoted as saying: "It's never been done before. There's never been a film of The Beatles actually at work. It'll all be there – the work, the breaks, everything. When the shooting is finished and the thing's been edited it will be offered for sale to world TV companies." Taylor said the concerts planned for Saturday the 25th would not take place, but there would be a performance of some kind. "The only thing I can say now is that it will take place, perhaps abroad." Asked about the rumoured North African amphitheatre gig, he replied: "There may now be some truth in this. It's an idea around at the moment, to do the shows abroad and take the fans along.

It would certainly be expensive, but an idea is to run some form of competition and take the winners."

There was disturbing news in other papers. *Disc & Music Echo* published Ray Coleman's recent interview with John Lennon, making a bold display quote out of his statement about Apple, which was heavily condensed as: "Apple is losing money. If it carries on like this we'll be broke in six months." The *Daily Sketch* had an inaccurate report about George and John's Twickenham altercation, in which Michael Housego wrote: "The awful tension of being locked up in each other's lives snapped the other night at a TV rehearsal and Beatles John and George swung, at very least, a few vicious phrases at each other." The reporter said he was aware that The Beatles "have been drifting apart as buddies, seeking strange new thrills, and frankly, getting on each other's nerves". He continued: "The activities of John Lennon and his Japanese girl friend Yoko Ono are in the public domain and it has not helped the others to rebuild the team as a friendly foursome. Lennon is completely immune to their criticism and there's not the slightest doubt in my mind that if he feels like taking his clothes off for the public again, he'll do it."

Both reports were sources of annoyance to The Beatles. John's loose words about Apple not only incensed Paul, but they pricked up the ears of the American businessman Allen Klein, who had been angling for a way into The Beatles' business for a while.

The *Daily Express* weighed in, bringing the fight story and the Apple story together in a report that denied the veracity of both, and quoting George as saying: "Apple has plenty of money – we all have. When John said we were losing money, he was talking about giving too much away to charities. We have been too generous and that's got to stop. The so-called punch-up between John and myself? There's no truth in it. We are still good friends." Ringo agreed that the punch-up didn't happen: "I was there when it was supposed to have taken place. It's quite untrue."

That Friday saw the release of the group's latest album, though its status as a new Beatles album was questionable. *Yellow Submarine*, the record of the film, included four substandard new songs, packaged with the title track (originally on *Revolver*), 'All You Need Is Love' and chunks of incidental music composed by George Martin. Critics complained that it was a heavily padded contractual-obligation long-player that could have been a decent four-track EP.

The following day, The Beatles' past came back to haunt them. Having filed a lawsuit against them claiming defamation of character, their former drummer Pete Best settled out of court for an undisclosed sum of money. During an interview with *Playboy* magazine in 1965, John and Paul had recalled how Ringo would fill in on drums when Pete was absent – which was true – but they had angered Pete by suggesting his absences were due to a pill-popping habit.

Not everybody was aware of the negative publicity The Beatles were attracting at the start of 1969. On Sunday, January 19, Cliff Richard made a telling public statement about the group. The pop star was singing hymns and discussing his Christian beliefs in front of hundreds of people at a church in Edinburgh when he suddenly declared: "The Beatles are very successful artists, and yet they are not successful in life. The Beatles do nothing but chase around the world after a dream, and they must now realise that their Maharishi just doesn't help them at all. I think they are looking for what Christians have found."

Aside from the fact that this was essentially just one religion knocking another, Cliff was behind the times. The Beatles' big Indian adventure had ended more than nine months before, and the last thing they could be accused of doing now was a "chase around the world". This statement from a music-business contemporary reveals just how low The Beatles' profile had become after they tucked themselves away for the *Get Back* sessions. Then again, some Beatles fans thought it was sour grapes because the group had long ago toppled Cliff from his dominant position as the UK's number one pop act.

The next day saw the inauguration of Richard Nixon as president of the USA. "I shall consecrate my office, my energies, and all the wisdom I can summon, to the cause of peace among nations," he vowed. He said he could see "the hope of tomorrow in the youth of today", adding: "I know America's youth. I believe in them. We can be proud that they are better educated, more committed, more passionately driven by conscience than any generation that has gone before."

But the consciences of many young Americans that day drove them to protest against their new Republican president. Thousands of demonstrators took part in a "counter-inaugural ball" in Washington, DC, setting up a green-and-white circus tent near the White House and swearing in a pig as their commander-in-chief. A London newspaper reported that "President-elect Nixon's motorcade into the heart of Washington had to be diverted when hippies threw nails across Independence Avenue and caused a traffic jam... Club-wielding police moved in on horseback, cracked skulls and repelled bands of rebels."

There were violent protests in Oxford that day, too, for a different reason. Enoch Powell was booked to speak at the city's town hall that evening, addressing members of Oxford University Conservative Association, and police intervened when pro-Powell and anti-Powell factions clashed outside the building. Socialists and anarchists marched through the city centre, chanting "Disembowel Enoch Powell!" According to *The Daily Telegraph*, "About 1,000 anti-Powell marchers, many of them students, linked arms and charged a three-deep cordon of 100 policemen at the town hall entrance. The cordon frequently bent under the weight of wave after wave of chanting, flag-waving demonstrators, but the line held as police helmets were sent flying." The "Rivers of Blood" politician was meanwhile escorted into the building via a side entrance, and after speaking he left by a back door as the scuffles continued.

When the *Get Back* sessions resumed in their new location on Wednesday, January 22, the atmosphere among The Beatles became less strained, partly because Apple's basement studio was a more intimate and friendly space than the cavernous studio in Twickenham. Paul Bond remembers being pleased to resume work on the production. "It had obviously been a wise decision to move," he says. "It certainly felt a lot cosier at Apple, and it was more sensible that they were working there. I always liked to get in early to the studio, because I had to load the films, get the cameras and stuff ready. And George was the only one who was ever there before me. He used to get in very early, and he'd be sitting there playing his guitar, practising and writing. And I'd make a cup of tea for him and a cup of tea for me."

When The Beatles assembled on that first day in the basement, they discussed some recent press stories, including the negative reports written about them. Cliff Richard's swipe at the group was dismissed by Ringo as "only Cliff doing his bit", but they were irritated by the Michael Housego article in the *Daily Sketch*, and John wondered if they could sue the reporter for libel. They laughed at a *Daily Telegraph* story highlighting public ignorance of current affairs. Asked in a survey about the identity of U Thant, some people had replied that he was "a pop singer" or "a submarine". In fact, U Thant was the Burmese diplomat who had now been secretary-general of the United Nations for more than seven years.

The atmosphere was further improved at the sessions by The Beatles becoming a quintet, with the unexpected addition of American keyboard player Billy Preston. Around mid-January, George remembered seeing Billy at the Royal Festival Hall four months before, and entertained the notion that he might make a valuable addition to The Beatles' sound. George had no idea where Billy was at that time; he might well have been back home in California. But it just so happened that Billy had been recording a special concert for BBC television on Sunday, January 19, at the Talk Of The Town, in the Hippodrome in London's West End, and he was also appearing on Lulu's TV show the following Saturday night.

"I knew Billy was in London," says Chris O'Dell, "but I'm not sure how – I think I was in touch with his agent. And I said something about Billy one day, and George said he'd like to see him. So I organised for Billy to come to Apple." He duly arrived soon after the group began their sessions in the basement, smiling his winning gap-toothed smile, and joined in on electric piano.

This was canny thinking from George, who knew that groups of well-acquainted people are much better behaved in the company of a relative stranger. The Beatles were aware that if they carried on bickering, individual members – particularly John and Paul – would give a negative impression of themselves to their new recruit. As George recalled years later, "He got on the electric piano, and straight away there was 100% improvement in the vibe in the room." George Martin called him an "emollient".

Bringing another musician in to play with The Beatles was a courageous move, perhaps reflecting George's increase in power after rejoining the group on the acceptance of his conditions. His confidence would also have been boosted by the fact that he had pulled a similar move successfully four months before. When Eric Clapton had come to play on 'While My Guitar Gently Weeps',

George had noticed the effect on John, Paul and Ringo: "It made them all try a bit harder; they were all on their best behaviour."

George was also acting on an instinct that Billy would be warmly received by his bandmates, which he was. Not only was he remembered as a friend from the Hamburg days, but also The Beatles knew and loved his 1965 album *Billy's Bag*, on which he played funky R&B Hammond-organ instrumentals. Now his cool and intelligent electric piano-playing gave their sound a lift, and they enjoyed the results.

The Beatles wanted a new instrument for Billy to play, and Paul specified a Fender Rhodes electric piano, well regarded among jazz and rock musicians for its distinctive mellow sound. The Fender company in America was alerted, and two pianos were loaded on to a transatlantic aircraft (John had added an extra piano to the order, for himself), but they were diverted to Sweden owing to foggy conditions in London. After they finally arrived at Apple, Paul realised that the Rhodes actually didn't make the sound he had imagined: he'd been thinking of a Wurlitzer. But, having spent around $8,000 and waited so long, they made do with it.

Between rehearsals of their new material, they were still fooling with cover versions, such as the thirties standard 'You Are My Sunshine', 'Milk Cow Blues' (as performed by Eddie Cochran and Elvis Presley), Chuck Berry's 'Little Queenie' and 'Queen Of The Hop' (a 1958 Bobby Darin hit). Sometimes the old and the new were mashed up, as when they started playing The Drifters' 'Save The Last Dance For Me' and suddenly burst into the chorus of 'Don't Let Me Down'. 'Dig A Pony' was still developing, with John discarding nonsense words and substituting new ones – a likely reason why, when it came to the public performance of the song, he wasn't able to recall the lyrics he had finally settled on. The words "Dig a pony" were fixed in place now, and phrases such as "Dig a skylight" and "Con a Lowry" had been tried and discarded.

John amused his colleagues with a mock stage announcement that renamed the song yet again. "I Dig A Pygmy, by Charles Hawtrey and the Deaf Aids," he proclaimed. "Phase one, in which Doris gets her oats." The lines were later slapped incongruously on the front of the *Let It Be* album, before the song 'Two Of Us'. Charles Hawtrey was a famous comic actor, known for his round "granny" spectacles, and a stalwart of the shifting team that appeared in the *Carry On* series of British film comedies. Hawtrey's original name was George Hartree, but he had adopted the name of a successful stage actor from the Victorian era. His most recent big-screen outing was *Carry On Up The Khyber*, released in 1968, in which he played Private Widdle.

After one performance of 'Dig A Pony', Paul joked that as a band, The Beatles improved with time like a fine wine, and compared them to a 1962-vintage Beaujolais.

On that first day down in the basement, The Beatles also returned to 'I've Got A Feeling', which was to be the second-most-played song of all their January sessions, after 'Get Back'. Instead of just discussing the previous evening's television viewing as they had done several times that month, they incorporated it into this song, with Paul and John giving impressions of the late Martin Luther King, whose "I have a dream" speech of 1963 had featured in an ITV documentary, *Deep South*. King would get another name-check, of sorts, during their final concert.

When *Melody Maker* hit the newsstands on Thursday, January 23, it reassured the music-buying public that all was well again in the Beatles camp. The foursome were now reconciled, it said, quoting an Apple spokesman (most likely Derek Taylor) as saying: "They are all friends again, together, strong as an ox as they have to be."

The paper's front-page lead story noted the increasing popularity of home-grown, blues-influenced rock music, confirming that The Beatles' plan to bring a raw, stripped-down sound to the world was in tune with the times. "Britain's blues-based groups are happening in America!" it screamed. "While Peter Green's Fleetwood Mac are still packing them in on their Stateside tour, Ten Years After this week became the first British blues or pop group to be invited to the world's top festival, the Newport Jazz Festival."

Fleetwood Mac's latest big hit was something of a departure for the band, however. 'Albatross', then at number two in the UK charts, was a blissful, swooning electric-guitar instrumental. The record was being kept off the top spot by a cover of The Beatles' 'Ob-La-Di, Ob-La-Da' by the Scottish band Marmalade. During the January sessions, Paul had noted with amusement that Marmalade had failed to use the word "bra" in the chorus as The Beatles had done.

Back in the basement at Apple on Thursday, January 23, the group made several more attempts at 'Get Back', and a sensible decision was made to drop the contentious verse about Pakistani immigrants. Billy Preston was now adding considerable musical interest to this simplistic song with flourishes of electric piano. John had opted to play lead guitar on the song, but was struggling with the quality of his playing.

The recordings from The Beatles' *Get Back* project would be extensively bootlegged, finding their way onto endless roughly packaged vinyl LPs and, ultimately, CDs, and the early references to "Pakistanis" in this song would be seriously misunderstood. People would miss the satire and accuse Paul McCartney of straightforward racism. Decades later, he was still defending lyrics he hadn't even included in the finished song. "There were a lot of stories in the newspapers then about Pakistanis crowding out flats – you know, living 16 to a room or whatever," he explained in 1986. "So in one of the verses of 'Get Back', which we were making up on the set of *Let It Be*, one of the outtakes has something about 'too many Pakistanis living in a council flat' – that's the line. Which to me was actually talking out against overcrowding for

Pakistanis... If there was any group that was not racist, it was The Beatles. I mean, all our favourite people were always black. We were kind of the first people to open international eyes, in a way, to Motown." Paul might also have added that The Beatles had consistently opposed the idea of playing concerts to segregated audiences in America, and that they refused to play in apartheid-era South Africa.

Thursday continued with The Beatles having a nostalgic but half-hearted go at 'I'll Get You', one of their B-sides from six years before, and Paul remarked that he thought he had Hong Kong flu – apparently a joke. John's sharp, ambiguous riposte was that he should take drugs.

Hong Kong flu was another of the big scare stories in the news at that time. It had made its first appearance in the British Crown colony (as it was then) in July 1968. The H3N2 virus responsible for the outbreak quickly spread to Singapore, Vietnam, the Philippines, India and Australia, and it entered the United States as a by-product of the Vietnam War, carried by American troops as they returned home. It had infected Britain by late 1968, and had now reached London. Most of the people affected by the pandemic suffered only mild symptoms, and British newspaper advertisements advised that if you were stricken with "Mao 'Flu'" you should take Aspro, the aspirin that "overpowers pain fast". However, the flu was fatal in thousands of cases. The Hollywood actress Tallulah Bankhead had died in December after suffering from H3N2, and the American double-bass player Paul Chambers, a sideman for jazz stars including Miles Davis and Thelonious Monk, was reported as a victim that January (though his cause of death was later believed to be tuberculosis).

West of Savile Row, in Charing Cross Road, a cautionary showbiz tale was unfolding as an American singing legend attempted a comeback. Judy Garland was playing a residency at the

Talk Of The Town, on the same stage where Billy Preston had recently performed for the BBC cameras. Due on every evening around 11.30 p.m., Judy was often late to appear, and sometimes failed to appear altogether. The star's health and voice had noticeably deteriorated, and she was drinking heavily and dosing up on amphetamines and barbiturates.

On January 19 the singer made an additional unscheduled TV appearance on *Sunday Night At The London Palladium*, filling in for the singer Lena Horne, who was unable to perform. Many viewers noticed that Judy appeared to forget the words to her first song, and telephoned the London Weekend TV studios to enquire and complain about it. Interviewed by a journalist the next day in her suite at the Ritz Hotel, Judy complained about having an "awful cold" and claimed that the fluffed lines were "all part of the act".

On the evening of Thursday, January 23, Miss Garland seriously tested the patience of the Talk Of The Town audience, who chanted and sang "Why are we waiting?" as midnight arrived without any sign of her. Dancers launched into an impromptu routine to placate them, and when Judy finally appeared, warbling 'I Belong To London', she was booed and had bread rolls, crackers and cigarette packets tossed at her. A heckler told her she ought to show some respect for the British public and appear on time, and the catcalls and jeering continued as she sang 'Get Happy' and 'Somewhere Over The Rainbow'. A man from the audience jumped on stage and grabbed her microphone, and after Judy announced that she'd had enough and walked off stage, someone hurled a glass that smashed behind her.

That Friday, Mal Evans was pleased to hear The Beatles busking the old Liverpool folk song 'Maggie Mae' in the skiffle style, and scribbled in his diary: "Beatles really playing together. Atmosphere is lovely in the studio – everyone is so much happier than of recent times." Before Billy Preston arrived for the session, John tabled the serious suggestion that Billy be allowed to join The Beatles as a permanent member – an idea that was gently vetoed by Paul. In a nostalgic mood later that day, they tried out some of their own juvenile compositions from the fifties, including the earliest song Paul ever wrote, 'I Lost My Little Girl' – sung by John in a Dylanesque vocal style – before returning to 'Get Back'.

They also romped through a selection of Chuck Berry songs, including 'Sweet Little Sixteen' and 'School Day'. Just over a mile away, in the Aldwych, there were scuffles as students protested outside the London School of Economics. The LSE had been a hotbed of student protest since 1966, when Dr Walter Adams was appointed as the college's director. Adams, previously the principal of the University College of Rhodesia, was seen by student activists as a supporter of the despised regime of white supremacist Ian Smith. Now the students were angered by steel security gates recently installed to allow parts of the LSE to be sealed off during protests. After they wrecked the gates using heavy tools, including sledgehammers, 25 students were arrested by police and the college building was closed.

That night, Judy Garland was unable to appear as billed at the Talk Of The Town. Stepping into her place was Lonnie Donegan, the British musician whose skiffle music had been inspirational to The Beatles in their youth.

That weekend was a potentially exhausting time for rock fans, bringing two super-long gigs of the kind that were popular in the late sixties. Dragging on for hours and featuring multiple bands, these events weren't routinely called "festivals" as they would be now, and were often staged indoors with minimal facilities. There was a "Midnite Rave" beginning after midnight on Friday at the Lyceum in London's Strand, which saw Status Quo sharing the bill with Joe Cocker, the blues-rock band Bakerloo Blues Line, and a trio called The Gun. The gig continued until 7 a.m. on Saturday, and advance tickets cost just £1. Even longer was the "non-stop pop concert" at Reading University on Sunday, clocking in at eight hours, though the bands were more obscure: The Liverpool Scene, Cannery Row, Modern Art Of Living and Levee Camp Moan. A short-lived rumour suggested that The Liverpool Scene were The Beatles playing under an alias, but knowledgeable punters knew they were a poetry band whose first album had been produced by the DJ John Peel.

More motivated now, and aware that Ringo didn't have many more days before he joined the production of *The Magic Christian*, The Beatles motored on into the weekend rather than taking a break. On the Saturday, their old Liverpudlian friend Cilla Black married her manager and longtime partner Bobby Willis in London while the group carried on toiling in the basement, trying out 'Two Of Us', 'For You Blue' and 'Let It Be'. With Cilla's devout Catholic parents absent from the Marylebone Register Office wedding, The Beatles' business manager, Peter Brown, gave the bride away. Bobby's best man was the tailor Tommy Nutter, soon to open his dazzling new shop in Savile Row, and the matron of honour was former *Ready Steady Go!* presenter Cathy McGowan. Cilla and Bobby held their reception at the Ritz, where Judy Garland was still in residence.

Romance was in the air again on Sunday, when Richard Burton splashed out £23,000 on a unique piece of jewellery for his wife, Elizabeth Taylor. Sotheby's auction house in London was selling La Peregrina, a weighty pear-shaped pearl with a serious history. Originally given by Philip of Spain in 1554 to his bride, Mary Tudor, Queen of England (and Henry VIII's daughter), it was subsequently worn by Spanish royalty and then taken by Napoleon Bonaparte's elder brother Joseph when he abdicated the Spanish throne in 1813. La Peregrina continued its travels (the reason for its name, "The Wanderer") when it was sold to a British aristocrat, the Duke of Abercorn, whose family had now put it up for sale.

The Burtons were in Las Vegas, where Elizabeth was being filmed for the movie *The Only Game In Town*, but her husband put in a remote bid for the pearl and won the auction, outbidding a Spanish prince keen to return it to his homeland.

Meanwhile, 1,400 miles east of Vegas, Elvis Presley entered American Studios in Memphis, Tennessee, to begin the recording sessions that would produce hits such as 'Suspicious Minds' and 'In The Ghetto'. He was clearly enjoying himself in the studio more than The Beatles were, telling the media: "As far as I'm concerned, this is the place to record. And the musicians here are fantastic."

Back in London, The Beatles' working Sunday began with George and Ringo arriving at Apple to find John and Paul both absent. George picked up his acoustic guitar and went through some recent compositions, performing 'Isn't It A Pity' and 'Let It Down', both of which would end up on *All Things Must Pass*. He also played the Harrison rarity 'Window, Window' – "I once knew a beautiful girl/She had long blonde hair in a curl..." – which would never be properly recorded, perhaps because he was unsure of its merits. Before demoing it again for producer Phil Spector the following year, he admitted it was "a bit silly". He may have disliked the rather vacant, window-gazing lyric, though the song's first 16 notes were infectious and promising.

Ringo tried out the number he had started writing in Sardinia, 'Octopus's Garden', and George went on the piano to help him develop it – a scene preserved in the *Let It Be* film. John and Yoko arrived in the basement as they progressed with the song. Ringo was now on piano, and when John asked what instrument he should play, Ringo laughed and suggested the drums. As the three Beatles played the number with John whacking the kit, Paul turned up, with Linda and her five-year-old daughter Heather in tow.

A series of loose jams and oldies later, John, back on guitar, began a spirited three-chord improvisation in the key of F, singing the title of Bob Dylan's 'Like A Rolling Stone' to a different tune before calling out a series of names of organisations and celebrities, creating another one of his "list songs", like the 'Get Off!' jam they had played 17 days earlier at Twickenham, in which he and Paul had traded lists of names. For this Sunday performance, the list included the FBI, CIA and BBC, as well as BB King, Doris Day and Matt Busby. Busby's name probably rolled off John's tongue because the Manchester United manager had announced 12 days before that he would be retiring at the end of the football season. John then repeated a phrase he had been using lately, "Dig it", and this off-the-cuff jam became part of Beatle history when an edited version was sequenced among the proper songs on the *Let It Be* album.

They enjoyed themselves with some old rock'n'roll numbers, including 'Blue Suede Shoes' and 'Lawdy Miss Clawdy', both of which Elvis had played during the informal jam section of his Comeback Special. More Beatle jams brought this Sunday session to an end, this time with Paul moving to Ringo's kit.

At some point that weekend, a momentous idea took shape at Apple HQ. Michael Lindsay-Hogg remembered that on the Saturday he lunched with The Beatles at the conference table: "Nice girls who did the cooking would bring in a first course, to be followed by roast chicken, vegetables and potatoes, with red and rosé wine, and something macrobiotic for John and Yoko." Michael was troubled by the structure of the film they were close to finishing, which had a beginning and a rather long middle, but no ending. He remarked that they needed to find a conclusion for the movie. There followed a debate with Yoko about whether conclusions were important or necessary, and Paul asked what sort of ending he would suggest.

Michael replied that they didn't have a big concert in Tunisia to serve as the finale, "smiling at George to signify no hard feelings (although they weren't quite soft yet)". But he had an idea for a place that might just work. "Why don't we do it on the roof?" he asked. Suggesting it made him feel like Mickey Rooney in one of the Andy Hardy movies, when he decides "We can put on the show right here." Michael was unsure that they'd go for the idea. "I put this forward believing that it could work but without a lot of confidence that they'd go for it. They were interested in their songs but I was interested in the film. To my surprise, they began to paw the idea, sniffing at it, knocking it from one to the other, to see if it was safe to take a bite. After lunch, Paul and Mal, Tony and I, Ringo, a few others, went up on the roof and had a look around. I was seeing where the cameras would go."

Cameramen captured the exploratory visit to the roof for posterity. In one shot taken by the *Get Back* project's stills photographer, Ethan Russell, we see Paul and Ringo standing at the back of the roof, surrounded by Glyn Johns, Michael Lindsay-Hogg, Kevin Harrington, Mal Evans and two cameramen: Les Parrott, pointing a hand-held movie camera, and Paul Bond, who was working as focus-puller on the camera.

There were small puddles on the roof from recent rain showers, and the surface must have looked uninviting to Paul, who made the practical suggestion that it be reinforced or shored up somehow to carry the group and all the equipment they needed. And they settled on the coming Wednesday as the big day for their concert on the roof.

Mal Evans had a slightly different memory of the idea's genesis, writing in 'Mal's Diary' for *The Beatles Book Monthly* that the idea for the rooftop concert came following lunch on the Sunday, "after we'd taken a breath of fresh air on the roof". In Michael's account, the idea was suggested by him over lunch downstairs; in Mal's version, they went up to the roof to take the air, and the lightbulb moment occurred there and then.

Glyn Johns' version, like Michael's, began with lunch at Apple but took a different course: "Ringo and I were in conversation about the building and its attributes and he asked me if I had ever been up on the roof, saying it had a wonderful view of the West End of London. So he took me and Michael Lindsay-Hogg up there, showing us a large area of flat roof with wonderful views of the city stretching away to the southwest. I suggested that if they wanted to play to a large crowd, why not play on the roof to the whole of the West End? We went back downstairs and put it to the others, and after some discussion it was agreed." That account, which involves only Glyn, Ringo and Michael, seems at odds with Ethan Russell's photograph from that weekend, which also shows Paul, Mal, Kevin and two cameramen – unless there was more than one roof sortie.

In yet another version, that of Billy Preston, the rooftop idea came from a different Beatle: "We were trying to figure out where we could have a concert, where everybody could come. So John came up with the brilliant idea to just play on the roof and play for everybody." Alternative accounts credit Ringo with the idea. Michael Lindsay-Hogg has joked that there are so many claimants to the rooftop idea that they include "the cook who made the apple crumble".

Michael wasn't aware that Jefferson Airplane had already played a rooftop gig in New York the previous month. "That December for me was really pretty busy," he explains. "We finished *Rock And Roll Circus*, then took a couple of days off, then I was starting to cut the *Circus* and also talking to The Beatles about the television special, and we decided we'd go in January. So I didn't have much else in my mind."

Ironically, although he had been dead set against a live performance, it was George Harrison's actions, more than those of his bandmates, that paved the way to the rooftop. Both of his stipulations in that January 15 meeting were crucial here: not only the cancellation of a grand official gig, but also the move to Apple. They didn't need to ask the permission of the building's owners to play on this roof, because they were the owners. That gave them the freedom and flexibility to be spontaneous, and it also offered them an ideal London location. If they had played a concert somewhere in Twickenham, it is likely to have required more planning and wouldn't have pulled the size or quality of the crowds they achieved in Mayfair. On top of all that, George helped to create The Beatles' "rooftop sound" by inviting Billy Preston to their January sessions.

As Monday dawned, with a new goal in clear sight, the group sharpened up their act, refining their slim pickings of new material so that it was gig-ready.

'Get Back' was in a decent, finished state, with all the lyrics present that would appear in the recorded version. Although it had been partly inspired by news stories about immigration, it had evolved into one of Paul's stock of "character" or "story" songs.

An instinctive songwriter, Paul often allowed his lyrics to develop in a euphonic way without any serious analysis of their meaning, tossing in names of characters to add colour and interest. Asked in 1976 about some of the words to his songs, he explained: "Somebody says, 'What did you mean by that?' and really I don't know. It just comes into your head... The whole meaning behind it starts to occur to you after you've written it. I suppose it's like going to a psychiatrist: you have a dream and you take it to the psychiatrist, and I suppose it's filled with meaning, but it's down to the psych to get it out. You just tell him you dreamed about walking round in your knickers, and he says, 'Well, this means...'

It's a bit the same with a song: you write a song in order to put some words to your tune; stuff just comes out... You hum along to your tune and something comes out, you start to get the idea."

Nearly 40 years later, he was still writing story songs and talking about them: "I think a lot of them, besides 'Eleanor Rigby', tend to be comedy. It's me doing the tongue-in-cheek thing, whereas 'Eleanor Rigby' was more serious. I think that's why it was more successful... It's quite a fun thing to do, to just dream up a name of a character and just try and write the story of that character and then make it fit with another character."

While he may have seized on the city of Tucson, Arizona, because Linda had been to university there, Paul has denied that the characters in 'Get Back' are based on real individuals. "Many people have since claimed to be the Jo Jo and they're not – let me put that straight! I had no particular person in mind: again it was a fictional character, half man, half woman, all very ambiguous. I often left things ambiguous. I like doing that in my songs."

Reasonably happy with their achievements in the basement, The Beatles decided there was still time for some larking about. Confident with 'Get Back' now, Paul launched into a playful foreign-language version, calling forth fragments of passable German that he recalled from the group's Hamburg days at the other end of the sixties. "*Geh weg!*" he sang ("go away"). "*Geh raus!*" ("get out"). He also added a little French towards the end. Another performance of the song, in English again this time, was so strong that it was used for the 'Get Back' single and the *Let It Be* album.

Mal Evans wrote in his personal diary that an engineer had visited the Apple building that Monday to inspect the load-bearing qualities of its flat roof, with the conclusion that it would support 5 pounds per square inch. Amplifiers, speakers and a Fender Rhodes piano, plus the weight of five grown musicians, a film director, cameramen and assorted technicians, would create a load of many hundreds of pounds, so measures were taken to reinforce it. Scaffolding was hired and erected across the roof, and wooden planks were ordered and fitted on top of the scaffolding, running parallel to the front and back of the building. In addition, metal poles were fitted beneath the roof.

Debbie Wellum was working in Apple's reception while the work was carried out. "My reception was littered with things like scaffolding and planks, and bags of tools. They hauled most of the planks up from the outside of the building." Taking no chances, Mal arranged for the roof to be reinforced not only on top, but from underneath as well. For several days, Chris O'Dell, trying to concentrate on her A&R work in her top-floor office, was continually distracted by the sounds of workmen erecting poles to provide additional support from below. The noise of the work, and the comings and goings of vans and strong men in overalls, did not go unnoticed by the Apple Scruffs and other fans hanging around The Beatles' headquarters that week.

On the Tuesday, the group continued with run-throughs of 'Get Back', 'Don't Let Me Down' and 'I've Got A Feeling'. They also played 'One After 909', and John recollected that he had offered the song once to The Rolling Stones, who hadn't been interested (the Lennon/McCartney song 'I Wanna Be Your Man' had a better reception, and became the Stones' second single). That day The Beatles also tackled two of George's compositions: 'Something', whose lyrics he was still struggling with, and 'Old Brown Shoe' (which would become the B-side of 'The Ballad Of John And Yoko', released in May that year).

John brought in a new gadget he had just discovered: a Stylophone, a small electronic, monophonic instrument whose flat 20-note metal keyboard was played with a stylus attached to the machine by a short wire. As George ran through the tricky chords of his song, other members of the band continued to fool around with the toy, leaving the vibrato switch on and playing off-key solos.

On the same day, John and Yoko had a meeting with Allen Klein in his suite at the swish Dorchester Hotel on Park Lane. Impressed by the tough-talking wheeler-dealer, John sent a message to EMI, saying that "from now on Allen Klein handles all my things". In early February, to Paul's displeasure, Klein would become the new Apple manager, sowing one of the seeds of The Beatles' break-up.

But now, on Tuesday, January 28, The Beatles had a more pressing concern. When they woke up the next day, they had a gig to play. They were set, as far as they were concerned, to play the roof. But Michael Lindsay-Hogg suddenly spotted a problem. "Tony Richmond and I looked at the weather projections on TV that night, because we had to get everything totally ready if we were going to shoot the next day. But the weather didn't look good enough: it was too gloomy. And then we woke up in the morning – the cameramen were on standby – and we saw that it was indeed very cloudy and very dull, so we pushed the shoot back a day. If the weather had been good enough, we were also going to use a helicopter for some aerial shots. But we certainly couldn't have used it on that day."

The idea of using a helicopter for the concert on Thursday was ultimately abandoned for legal reasons. As Mal Evans wrote, "We'd have loved to get a helicopter shot to show both the fellows on the roof and the crowd in the street but the law won't let you fly one over London and it was too late to borrow a balloon!"

"Whether there was an air-traffic problem with using a helicopter I don't know," says Michael, "but it may have been that we were told we couldn't do it. Lots of times in that period, you had the idea and you went forward with it as much as you could, until someone told you, 'You actually can't do this. You'll be arrested!'"

The Beatles continued their rehearsals in the basement. During a long conversation with John, even as the rooftop concert was looming, Paul was still advocating the idea of the group performing their new songs in front of the cameras in a studio or theatre. Mal Evans told Paul he had just had a dream about The Beatles playing a fantastic show, and this was something Paul still hankered after: they could play to an invited audience at the Saville Theatre, he suggested. But, as when Paul had criticised George's playing back at Twickenham, Paul was listening to himself again and disliking the way he sounded: like someone badgering the group to make a Judy Garland-style comeback.

With 885 days separating Thursday's performance from their last concert at Candlestick Park, they were unaccustomed to playing live and were nervous about doing it again. Paul reminisced about how jittery they had been when they played concerts back in the early sixties, but how the feeling had waned with subsequent performances. His message was that the only way to conquer their nerves was to play more gigs.

After a day of lacklustre rehearsals, The Beatles talked optimistically with Michael Lindsay-Hogg about the big plan for the next day. George, who seemed to have an offbeat vision of how the rooftop concert would look, asked Michael if he was still expecting them to be "on the chimney with a lot of people" the following day. The director, who had been through so many abortive discussions about unrealised concerts, joked that he didn't use the word "expecting" any more. But like the others, George sounded upbeat about the imminent event. He was fine with it — he'd do it.

CHAPTER FOUR

Up On The Roof

Dawn broke almost imperceptibly over the West End of London on Thursday, January 30, 1969. The overlapping clouds, in varying shades of grey, were so thick that they allowed only a glimmer of sunlight to penetrate. Every so often, as the clouds shifted like airborne tectonic plates, a patch of greyish-blue sky became visible, only to be obscured minutes later.

It was dry, and not terribly cold; late December had been much worse, with Arctic winds, blizzards and deep snow drifts causing disruption in much of Britain. The month of January had been relatively mild, though the wind was brisk today, blowing at more than 11 miles per hour, creating a significant wind-chill factor. Most of the people in the streets early that morning were wrapped up in coats, scarves and gloves as the west-southwesterly wind whipped up Piccadilly, Pall Mall and Shaftesbury Avenue, and gusts funnelled into narrower thoroughfares including Duke Street, St James's Square, Wardour Street and Savile Row, blowing sweet wrappers, cigarette butts and the other litter of the previous evening around.

The gloom was punctuated by the headlights of a few early-morning vehicles on the roads, orange lights on top of taxis and lights in the windows of offices being cleaned ready for the influx of staff. Electric light spilled from sleepy Mayfair hotels, the Ritz on Piccadilly, Brown's on Albemarle Street and Claridge's on the corner of Brook and Davies Streets, and the lights were on in West End Central, the main police station in Savile Row, near the junction with Burlington Street, as uniformed officers went about their business.

The police would intervene in The Beatles' rooftop concert much earlier than most people imagine. In fact, they came close to scuppering it before it had begun. Up in the Chiltern Hills, to the north-west of London, Dave Harries and another technical engineer, Keith Slaughter, were leaving Dave's home in the market town of Chesham and driving to Savile Row. The previous day they had paid a visit to the studios at EMI in Abbey Road, collecting the best amplification equipment they could find for the open-air show and loading it into a vehicle from the EMI carpool, and now they were motoring towards the capital through the early-morning gloom.

"It was really early, about four o'clock in the morning," remembers Dave, "and we looked really dodgy, because we had ropes and speakers and amps in the back, and we were all dressed up in big coats with hats and scarves. And suddenly the police pulled us over. We must have looked like burglars, I suppose. They said, 'Where are you going?' But the concert was all hush-hush, and we weren't supposed to say anything about it. We said we were sorry, but we couldn't tell them where we were going. We told them it was a film shoot and that we were working for EMI Records. And fortunately, it wasn't Keith's car, it was an EMI pool car, so Keith said, 'If you check the ownership of this vehicle, you'll find it's an EMI pool car.' Which they did, and they let us go. Had we told them what we were doing, what it was all about, they might have stopped everything at that point."

Arriving in Savile Row after their close shave, Dave and Keith unloaded the gear, including several speakers, hauled everything to the roof and began setting it up with the help of Alan Parsons. "The speakers were on stands and could be swivelled downwards," says Dave, "and we positioned them at the front of the roof, facing the street, and we had as many power amps as we could get. We were trying to make it as noisy as possible." Down in the basement, they connected three recording desks and ran long cables all the way up to the roof, and checked that everything was working.

Down at street level, the signs outside London's darkened theatres promised a rich mix of entertaining shows, whose stars were currently slumbering in theatrical digs and hotel rooms. As you travelled down Shaftesbury Avenue, there was *Hair*, still packing people in at the Shaftesbury Theatre. At the Saville Theatre, which Brian Epstein had leased not long ago for a series of rock concerts, there was *Queen Passionella And The Sleeping Beauty*, a "Pantomime Extraordinaire" starring the female impersonator Danny La Rue in the lead role – a show that, according to one reviewer, was "not only unsuitable but, to judge from the few I saw around me, deeply boring for small children".

The Queen's Theatre was staging *The Servant Of Two Masters*, a modern adaptation of an 18th-century Italian comedy, starring the pioneering British rock'n'roll star Tommy Steele as the hapless servant Truffaldino. The nearby Globe had *There's A Girl In My Soup*, a romantic farce starring Jon Pertwee and Donald Sinden, which for a while would hold the record as London's longest-running comedy stage show.

Two old Liverpudlian friends of The Beatles were also treading the boards here. The Adelphi in the Strand was presenting the hugely popular musical comedy *Charlie Girl*, starring Gerry

Marsden of Gerry & The Pacemakers, while the London Palladium had the pantomime *Jack And The Beanstalk*, starring the comedian Jimmy Tarbuck as the boy who trades a cow for some magic beans. Jimmy had attended the same primary school as John Lennon, and when John had played Jimmy The Beatles' first record, 'Love Me Do', he told John he should sell the song to The Everly Brothers – a remark that the Beatle would often laughingly throw back in the comedian's face after his group had become global superstars.

Over at the Ambassadors near Cambridge Circus, Agatha Christie's *The Mousetrap* was already in its "17th inexorable year", and still pleading with its audiences not to reveal the play's surprise twist ending to anybody. Further south at the Victoria Palace Theatre, opposite Victoria Station, *The Black And White Minstrel Show* somehow continued to entertain thousands of punters, with its white male performers "blacking up" to play grotesquely offensive caricatures of African-American singers. In 1967 the Campaign Against Racial Discrimination had delivered an unsuccessful petition to the BBC asking for the Minstrels' massively popular TV show to be taken off air.

The traffic picked up as the early car commuters began arriving, and muffled car radios could be heard playing classical music broadcast by BBC Radio 3 and pop music on Radio 1. Fleetwood Mac's sedate, blissed-out 'Albatross', number one in the charts, was played at regular intervals, and other discs on heavy rotation were Stevie Wonder's 'For Once In My Life', Martha Reeves & The Vandellas' 'Dancing In The Street', The Move's 'Blackberry Way' and Sandie Shaw's 'Monsieur Dupont'.

Distributors were hefting thousands of bundles of newspapers and magazines for delivery to newsagents' shops and street vendors. The latest edition of *The Times* reported that the government was "throwing its full weight" behind university authorities to end the current spate of student agitation. The LSE was still closed, and two of its lecturers were to be investigated for their possible collusion in the recent violent protests there. Edward Short, the secretary of state for education and science, had raised the idea that student grants could be withheld from some of the troublemakers. "It is high time," he said in Parliament, "that one or two of these thugs are thrown out on their necks."

There was another delay to the maiden flight of Concorde, the new supersonic airliner created by Britain and France. It had been supposed to take off in 1968, but its assembly had taken longer than expected. The latest delay was due to overheating of the disc brakes, but it looked as if the plane would finally get off the ground later that year.

That week's edition of *Melody Maker* informed its readers that the guitarist Trevor Burton had left The Move, forcing the group to cancel an American tour due to begin that day. "Musical policy is the reason for the split. Burton wants to play blues and is to join another Birmingham group, the Uglys. The rest of the group prefer to concentrate on more commercial pop music." Unlikely as it may seem, Hank Marvin, The Shadows' bespectacled lead guitarist, had been invited to replace Burton, but declined.

At 8 a.m. sharp, PC Ken Wharfe took his assigned position at Piccadilly Circus. The 19-year-old bearded policeman was on traffic duty at a pedestrian point there, wearing special white cuffs to direct traffic and help pedestrians cross the road. Another policeman took up his position at the junction of Piccadilly and Shaftesbury Avenue. Early commuters were arriving in town by bus, train and tube to start their day's work. Many wore heavy overcoats, while others wore beige or grey raincoats, because "occasional showers" had been forecast for later in the day.

The occasional milk float trundled along, its crates of pint bottles rattling. But the streets were a little quieter than on a normal Thursday because there were no Royal Mail vans picking up and delivering letters and parcels. There were no collections today from red pillar boxes, some of which were jammed full of envelopes, and sacks of mail were forming miniature mountains in sorting offices. Postal workers were on strike, and instead of serving customers and sorting and delivering mail, many of them were preparing to take their grievances to the street. They were preparing to march through London, and were sticking crudely printed slogans onto placards: "We demand a fair deal", "Low pay leads to lack of staff" and "Blame the Post Office – not us!" The big Post Office in Trafalgar Square was normally open 24 hours a day and bustling with activity, but today it was empty, locked and as silent as a grave.

The strike was a gesture of solidarity with thousands of foreign-based telegraphists – staff who took and relayed messages by telegram, cable and Telex – demanding a higher pay rise than the 7% the government had offered. The telegraphists were also losing overtime pay because of mechanisation and receiving scant compensation. London was just one of 19 British cities with piles of mail going nowhere that day.

The tailors of Savile Row would soon open for business, their workshops buzzing with industry as craftsmen took sharp shears to exquisite fabrics to make beautiful suits for businessmen, celebrities, aristocrats and royalty. Over at No. 3, work had begun earlier than usual, and Debbie Wellum was already at her desk in reception. "We were all told to come in early, and The Beatles came in early as well. It was bloomin' freezing cold, and George was in his black furry coat. I think Ringo was the last to arrive, and none of them looked particularly happy."

Michael Lindsay-Hogg travelled in to Savile Row from Parliament Hill Road in Hampstead. He and his girlfriend, the actress Jean Marsh, were staying in a ground-floor flat borrowed from one of Jean's friends, the Liverpudlian actor Norman

Rossington, who was away filming. Connoisseurs of trivia may note that this provides a link between The Beatles' final film and their first, *A Hard Day's Night*, in which Norman had played the role of Norm, the group's road manager.

The early-morning start at Apple was to ensure that everything was ready for the concert, and there was much to do. Cameras, sound equipment and lighting had to be set up by engineers inside the building, including a hidden camera to film any policemen who came through the front door later that day. The camera was placed inside a tall box in a corner of the reception area; the box was painted white to match the walls, and the camera lens was concealed by a two-way mirror.

There was a beautiful, professionally made cushion flower arrangement on a table in reception, and a microphone was hidden inside to record any interesting conversations that might occur. Debbie herself was wired for sound as well: "They stuffed a microphone up my skirt," she laughs, "and concealed it in my top. I suppose they put it up my skirt to conceal the wiring."

As usual, there were Apple Scruffs loitering outside the building. These extreme Beatles devotees formed an exclusive club, which had its own magazine, and followed their idols from place to place – from Apple to Abbey Road, Trident Studios or Cavendish Avenue. "I built up quite a relationship with the Scruffs when I was there," says Debbie. "They were lovely girls and they were very respectful, but they were always at the office before the first person arrived, and always at the office when everybody left – except for if The Beatles were recording, and then they'd be at the studios. And they would almost tell *us* where The Beatles were."

The Scruffs were quick to realise that something unusual was happening at No. 3 Savile Row – they had seen delivery vehicles and people coming and going – and that there was more activity than usual. It wasn't just the Scruffs: other devoted fans were wise to it all as well. "There were a few of us who knew something was happening," recalls Paula Marshall. "There had been stuff coming out of a van and going in." Paula was 16 and worked as an office junior at an advertising agency in the West End, but that Thursday she had skipped work, coming in by tube from her home in Walthamstow in the East End and making a beeline for Savile Row.

Paula had been a fan since 1962, when she heard 'Love Me Do' while returning from a week-long school trip to Colomendy in the North Wales countryside. "I remember thinking, 'I like that,' and that was the beginning of the whole thing for me. The first record I bought was 'I Want To Hold Your Hand' in 1963. I bought it at Woolworth's for six shillings and eightpence and walked out with it in a bag, feeling very proud."

The Beatles would be using many microphones on the Apple roof that day – not just for the vocals, but also over the drums and to pick up the sound of their amplifiers. The engineer Glyn Johns saw how gusty it was and became concerned that the microphones would be battered by the wind and pick up a lot of unwanted noise, spoiling the recordings of the songs. He decided that the mikes should be covered by a special gauzy fabric that would filter out the air turbulence from the music, and instructed the most junior member of the team, 20-year-old Alan Parsons, to go and purchase some. "Glyn asked me to go out and buy some ladies' stockings to drape over the mikes," Alan later recalled. He dutifully trooped off to Marks & Spencer on Oxford Street, where the staff raised a few eyebrows and asked him what size of stockings he required. "I said, 'It really doesn't matter.' So they thought I was either going to rob a bank, I think, or I was a cross-dresser!"

As it happened, it was actually a very good day to rob a bank. At 12.00 noon sharp, hundreds of clerks working in London's banks simultaneously withdrew their labour and walked out of their workplaces, leaving many banking branches understaffed. The bankers were aggrieved at the decision of the Labour government to block their latest pay rise. Many of them were earning around £1,000 or £2,000 a year, and male clerks had been due to receive a 7% increase, while women had been in line for an 11% raise, but the salary hikes had been referred to the Prices & Incomes Board. Many branches insisted that they would soldier on with a "skeleton staff", and senior banking staff took over the counters that day. Some of the clerks went to lobby their MPs at the House of Commons, while others went home or amused themselves in London.

Disgruntled men and women from the Post Office, wrapped up in long coats and carrying their placards, marched through the streets towards Hyde Park, with police officers accompanying them to maintain order. About 10,000 massed in Hyde Park and cheered as Tom Jackson, the generously moustached leader of the Union of Post Office Workers, criticised the government's ill treatment of overseas telegraph workers and discussed the possibility of extending the strike. The rally was orderly but noisy: there was chanting and singing, and some demonstrators played instruments such as guitars, banjos, drums and bagpipes.

Barbara Bennett, who worked at Apple as secretary to Neil Aspinall, left 3 Savile Row to lunch that day with her best friend, the company's telephonist Laurie McCaffrey, who was well known at Apple for her sonorous voice, Liverpudlian accent and astonishing efficiency. They walked to Piccadilly Circus and to one of their favourite lunchtime haunts, Billy's Baked Potato. This was part of a small chain run by the famous boxer Billy Walker and his entrepreneurial brother George, which offered honest-to-goodness, school-dinnerish food at very reasonable prices. "You had to queue there, because it was so popular," says Barbara. "As well as baked potatoes, you could have things like bananas and custard."

There was a sense of expectation among the few fans gathered in Savile Row. "We knew it wouldn't be long before something happened," says Paula Marshall, "because The Beatles' roadies were there. We knew them and they knew us; it was like a little family."

The group's "chief roadies" during their touring days, in charge of transporting all their equipment and setting it up on stage, were Mal Evans and Neil Aspinall. After The Beatles stopped playing live concerts, both remained in the band's employ, and they had now gravitated to jobs at Apple – Mal as the group's personal assistant, and Neil as the company's managing director. Helping Mal these days was Kevin Harrington, who had originally come into The Beatles' orbit as Brian Epstein's office boy, but had also moved over to Apple.

That day, Neil Aspinall was absent: he had suddenly come down with tonsillitis, and was in hospital having the offending tonsils removed. "Neil and I were the best of friends; he was a wonderful man," says Peter Brown. "He asked me to be his best man at his wedding. He and I just got on so well together. He did the artistic side and I did all the administrative side, but we just liked each other. And when they decided to play on the rooftop and he suddenly got sick, I was very concerned."

It was down to Mal and Kevin to set up all the group's instruments that day. Their task was to carry all the guitars, drums, amplifiers, microphones and Billy Preston's electric piano all the way up from the basement to the top floor, and then up to the roof. The space inside the lift was extremely limited, so they made several journeys with the equipment. On reaching the top floor, they had to carry the gear out of the lift and up a spiral staircase to the roof. The largest items were Paul's bass speaker cabinet and Billy's piano. The piano, a Fender Rhodes Seventy-Three Silver Sparkle Top Suitcase model, could be easily divided into two parts – the keyboard section simply lifted out of the cabinet – but it was still a substantial and very heavy piece of equipment.

"The piano and the bass cabinet were huge," recalls Kevin, "and I couldn't get the cabinet round the turn at the top of the stairs. It just wouldn't go. I told Mal, and he suggested we take it through the skylight instead. So he unscrewed the frame of the skylight – he made quick, short work of it – and we were able to force it through there. We got Billy's piano through there as well. What The Beatles wanted, The Beatles got!"

Kevin says he wasn't selective about the instruments he hauled to the roof. "I didn't know which songs they were going to play, and as far as I remember, I just took all the stuff I could from the basement studio." John would be playing his beloved Epiphone Casino hollow-bodied guitar, George had his custom-made Rosewood Telecaster and Paul would play a classic Höfner violin bass. This still had the 1966 setlist taped to its body, and the "Bassman" sticker that he had slapped on during the rehearsals. Ringo would play his new Hollywood maple-finish drum kit. Everything went up except an acoustic piano, which would have been too big and heavy to shift manually. "There's no way you could have carried that up there. You would have had to use a big crane or a helicopter to do that," says Kevin. Some of the gear laid out on the roof would not be used, such as John's lap steel guitar and a Hohner electric piano.

They would surprise a great many people that day. "The roof show was supposed to be a complete surprise: we thought that would be part of the fun," says Michael Lindsay-Hogg. But there were a select few people, apart from the employees of Apple, who knew the concert was going to happen, because they had been invited. Tony Richmond, the director of photography for the TV special, had invited his fiancée, Linda DeVetta, who had been the make-up artist on Godard's *Sympathy For The Devil*, and on

Michael's promo film for the Stones' 'Jumpin' Jack Flash'. Michael had invited his girlfriend, Jean Marsh*. He had also tipped off his friend Vicki Wickham, who had been the producer of *Ready Steady Go!* when he had worked on the show. Vicki was now writing for the music papers, and would soon leave London to run the New York office of Track Records, the label set up by the managers of The Who.

Vicki left her home in the middle of New Cavendish Street to come to Savile Row that lunchtime and see The Beatles' performance, and she brought two friends with her: Cathy McGowan, the famous presenter of *Ready Steady Go!*, and Rosemary Simon. "Rosemary was my personal assistant at the time, and she was much younger than me," says Vicki. "She came from a very posh family. She was a wonderfully efficient worker, and the other thing that was great about her was that she had a car, which was very useful! She later married Paul Samwell-Smith of The Yardbirds and became a lawyer."

As Vicki, Cathy and Rosemary walked down Savile Row from Conduit Street around midday, there were few signs that anything special was about to happen. Having been admitted to No. 3, they went up in the lift and climbed to the roof. "And there was Michael, a great friend of all of us, standing there with a cigar in the freezing cold. He said we could stand at the side of the roof, against the wall, if we wanted to, but that we might get a better view of the concert if we went up to another roof on the opposite side of the road."

Directly opposite Apple HQ in those days was the Royal Bank of Scotland, and the trio entered the building and were somehow allowed to take the lift to the roof, where they found they had an

---

* In 1971 Marsh would co-create and star in the enormously popular, award-winning period TV series *Upstairs, Downstairs*, about the lives of the servants and masters in a grand house in Belgravia.

excellent view of the roof of No. 3 across the road. "I can't remember what we sat on, but we sat down on something."

A 19-year-old American called Leslie Samuels was living in London at the time, studying journalism at the London College of Printing, at Elephant and Castle. As president of the New York chapter of the Beatles USA fan club, she had contacts at Apple, and had been alerted to the possibility of a special event that day. "I was living off Rutland Gate at the time, near Hyde Park, so it was really easy to hop on the bus to Piccadilly and walk from there to Savile Row. I was walking my dog, Brian, who was a big bearded collie."

Leslie had already accumulated an enviable collection of Beatle experiences. Not only had she seen the group play Washington, DC, Philadelphia, Boston and Shea Stadium as a 16-year-old in 1966, but she had also met three of The Beatles when she came to England the following year. She visited Paul and George at their respective homes – Paul let her hold his two small kittens – and wrote about the experiences for *Teen Datebook* magazine. "When I met John, I was thinking, oh God, I hope he's not ugly to me. But he wasn't – he was very thoughtful. It was the summer of love and flowers, and I brought a little bouquet of flowers for him – which is what I did when I met Paul and George as well. We were talking by his front door in Weybridge, where he had just taken possession of his famous psychedelic Rolls-Royce, and he said, 'Oh, it's in the garage. Do you want to see it?' And he opened the door to his garage, and said I could go and sit inside it if I wanted. So I did."

As Leslie arrived at Savile Row, wearing a red leather coat that protected her from the cold wind, she saw some familiar faces. "There were half a dozen Apple Scruffs there, who I recognised because they were often there. I wasn't as committed to just hanging around the building like that; I couldn't do that, because I had a life and I was going to college."

Staff at *New Musical Express* had advance notice of The Beatles' performance as well, only because Mavis Smith, who worked in Apple's press office, was married to *NME* writer Alan Smith. "Word went out that The Beatles were doing it," says Keith Altham, who was also writing for *NME*, "and we were asked if we wanted to go along and catch a bit of it. So about three of us hopped out of the office and went along." It was a short trip west from the paper's offices in Long Acre, Covent Garden, to Savile Row.

Many Apple staff members were disappointed to hear that they weren't allowed to go up on the roof to hear The Beatles play. Although it had been reinforced from above and below, there were still concerns about how many people it would support, and only "essential staff" were allowed up there. Tony Richmond found 21-year-old Chris O'Dell moping in her top-floor office because she wouldn't see the show, and suggested she go up with him as his "assistant". She grabbed her coat and tagged along.

The Beatles were using one of the small Apple offices as a makeshift dressing room, discussing the songs they should play and in what order they could play them. The stage fright they had discussed recently was very much in evidence. Ken Mansfield, head of the Apple label in the USA, walked into the office and "saw before me a young group of rockers going over their set and showing signs of nervousness and pre-stage jitters just like any other band".

Around 12.20, Michael Lindsay-Hogg joined John, Paul, George and Ringo as they were still preparing – or so it initially seemed – to walk out onto the roof and begin the show. George was questioning the point of going up on the roof and playing, and Ringo complained that it was very cold up there. Typically keen, Paul urged the others to do it, assuring them that it would be "fun", but John – as he had been doing lately – was choosing not to take part in the conversation.

There was a worrying moment when it looked as if the rooftop would go the way of Tunisia, Greece, Libya, the Grand Canyon, the National Gallery, the House of Commons, Liverpool Cathedral and all the other places they had considered and ultimately rejected. "Suddenly I realised there was a problem," recalls Michael. "The plan wasn't secure at all."

After an agonising silence, John Lennon suddenly came through as the leader of the group, as he had been from the beginning. "Fuck it. Let's do it," he said. With John on side, George and Ringo immediately dropped their objections, and within minutes all four Beatles climbed up the spiral staircase, one by one, to play music together in public for the final time.

Paul McCartney walked tentatively out of the rooftop door, eyeing the view from the roof, dressed in a dark suit over a striped shirt, much of his face insulated from the cold by his bushy beard. He jumped up and down on the wooden planks, getting a feel for the surface of their new makeshift stage.

Ringo Starr came out on the roof with his wife, Maureen, who had lent him the orangey-red coat that was giving him some protection from the weather. He parked himself on the drum stool and picked up his sticks. Billy Preston, in a black leather jacket, took up his position behind the electric piano, stage right. George Harrison came out, then John with Yoko. George wore bright green trousers and a shaggy black coat. John, in gold-rimmed glasses, was wearing dark trousers and a dark zip-up top, and was wrapped in the brown fur coat that had been a fixture at recent public appearances. He had been overdressed when he had worn it in the summer of 1968, but today he would benefit from its warmth. All of The Beatles would be glad of their luxuriant, thick hair today.

Yoko and Maureen each found a place to sit against the chimney on the side of the roof nearest No. 2, which was the building occupied by the wool merchants Wain, Shiell & Son. They were next to two Americans: Ken Mansfield, in an inadequately thin and unlined white raincoat, and Chris O'Dell. There was no warmth coming up the chimney, but it was big enough to give them some shelter from the wind.

Keith Altham of *NME* had a playful conversation with John Lennon after mounting the stairs to the roof. "I was shivering like a lunatic in my jacket, and John came up to me and asked if I wanted to borrow his fur coat. And before I could say yes, he said, 'Tough!' Typical John."

The three guitar-playing Beatles had chopped and changed their stage positions over the years. Usually the audience would see Paul on the left, and in some shows they saw John to the right of him and then George on the far right, but in other shows John and George might switch positions, or George might be to the far left. They might also vary their positions during a single show, as various Beatles shared a microphone for a particular song. Today they assembled in one of their classic formations from the early sixties: Paul, John, George, with Ringo visible at the back in the space between Paul and John, and with the addition of Billy at the back to the far left.

The first loud noises heard from the roof that day were John, Paul and George tuning their guitars. They had a brief sound check, trying out 'Get Back'; then they launched into the song again with more conviction. It was the first time the public had ever heard the new number, and they heard it coming directly from a high roof, and as a stream of ricochets from various buildings and different directions.

Leslie Samuels, with her comprehensive knowledge of The Beatles' music, realised that she had never heard 'Get Back' before. "I was talking to people and I remember saying, 'Wow! This is new stuff.'"

Alistair Taylor decided to watch the show from the street, enjoying the atmosphere of the event among the crowd on a corner of Savile Row. Another Apple employee, Jean Nisbet, left her office for the street after the ceiling of her office began to vibrate alarmingly with the music.

Unlike the privileged invitees, most of those who witnessed the rooftop concert had no prior notice of it, and simply had the good fortune to be in the right place at the right time. A 20-year-old art student called Steve Lovering was having lunch round the corner with a friend, Brian Wakefield, who was a student at the Royal Academy of Arts in Piccadilly. "I was living in Kensington and studying at the Maidstone School of Art in Kent at the time, in my third year," says Steve, "and I was in London that day to see a couple of exhibitions and grab some lunch with Brian at the Royal Academy, which had a pretty good refectory in the basement. We were sitting there when suddenly we heard all this noise. It sounded like someone tuning up and doing a sound check, and you could hear the sound really loudly in that refectory. There were people complaining and tutting. But I said, 'Fuck! I know what this is – I'm going round there!' Because I knew where the Apple building was.

"So I rushed out the side entrance of the Academy and ran round the corner – I think I was still holding a bun in my hand, and I was wearing a reefer jacket like the one worn by Paul McCartney on their 'Long Tall Sally' EP. My friend Brian wasn't a fan, so he stayed behind in the refectory. And they kicked off with 'Get Back' and it was just amazing. It was obvious that it was The Beatles: they just had that distinctive sound. There weren't many people there in the street when it all started, but then gradually more and more people stopped, and a crowd started to form."

Although the event has gone down in history as "The Beatles' rooftop concert", that's really a misnomer. They were on the roof for two reasons: to record live versions of several songs for their album, and to provide a climactic ending to the film they were making, at the suggestion of Michael Lindsay-Hogg. It's probably too late now to amend the nomenclature for the annals, but this was really "The Beatles' rooftop recording session" – hence the multiple attempts they made at 'Get Back' and other songs. Mal Evans confirmed this with a description of the event in one of the diary pieces he wrote for *The Beatles Book Monthly*: "One particular day's work at the end of January caused quite a stir. To get something a bit different, an open-air sound, we shifted the session from the basement studio to the roof of 3 Savile Row!" It was an unusual recording session, though, in that it had a live audience.

And The Beatles certainly wanted an audience: they and their director had deliberately chosen the lunchtime period for the performance, because they were likely to draw much bigger crowds around that time than mid-morning or mid-afternoon (by the evening it would have been too dark to play). In fact, it's clear that Paul, at least, was expecting a much stronger audience reaction to the music. As they finished that version of 'Get Back', they were rewarded with some polite clapping. This must have sounded absurd after all the ear-piercing screaming of the Beatlemania years, and Paul was reminded of the muted behaviour of crowds at test match cricket, quipping: "It looks like Ted Dexter has scored another."*

---

* By 1969, 33-year-old Ted Dexter was actually a fading star on the cricket scene, but he was still remembered for his dynamic captaincy of the England and Sussex teams in the early sixties.

Savile Row c.1960. Wool merchants Wain, Shiell & Son (No. 2, with the long flagpole) complained bitterly to the police when The Beatles played on the roof next door in 1969. (Popperfoto/Getty Images)

Paul meets his future wife Linda Eastman for the second time, at the press launch for *Sergeant Pepper's Lonely Hearts Club Band*, on 19 May, 1967. (John Downing/Getty Images)

The debonair Peter Brown helped The Beatles put Apple together, and dealt with the police on the famous rooftop. (Mirrorpix)

George and Pattie Harrison at the opening of the Apple Boutique in Baker Street, December 1967. (Terry O'Neill/Iconic Images)

John Lennon attended the opening party with his wife Cynthia. (Terry O'Neill/Iconic Images)

Friends including Cilla Black arrived to toast the new venture. (Terry O'Neill/Iconic Images)

John and Paul arrive in New York in May 1968 to publicise the launch of Apple.
With them are Mal Evans (centre) and the Greek electronics wizard Magic Alex (left).
(Fred W. McDarrah/Getty Images)

John and Paul return to London
after the publicity bash.
(Stroud/Express/Getty Images)

Lennon and McCartney with
their publicist Derek Taylor (right)
and business manager
Peter Brown (behind desk).
(Jane Bown/Observer/TopFoto)

John with Yoko Ono, 1968.
The brown fur coat would later keep him warm
during the rooftop concert.
(Mirrorpix)

Six months before the rooftop concert, the Apple Boutique closes down and gives its stock away to lucky shoppers.
(left: Bob Aylott/Keystone/Getty Images) (right: C. Maher/Express/Getty Images)

George at Apple Corps in 1968. The youngest Beatle's brief departure from the group in January 1969 was a key factor in the events that led to the rooftop concert. (Baron Wolman/Iconic Images)

George, Ringo, Yoko, John and Paul (left to right) listen to a playback in Apple's basement studio in Savile Row, where they resumed the 'Get Back' project in late January 1969. (Trinity Mirror/Mirrorpix/Alamy)

Billy Preston and Lulu, on Lulu's BBC TV show broadcast on 25 January, 1969.
Billy would play electric piano on the roof with The Beatles five days later.
(Michael Putland/Getty Images)

The Beatles play the rooftop at lunchtime on Thursday, 30 January, 1969.
Towering over them here is the director Michael Lindsay-Hogg. (Camera Press/RBO)

Paul McCartney plays a high-rise gig in New York City in 2009, 40 years after the rooftop concert. (Ray Tamarra/Getty Images)

The Beatles' rooftop gig has inspired many artworks, including this model by Bob Bartey and Dave Loboda.

Crafted using a variety of household objects, it is still a work in progress. (both photographs: Bob Bartey/Dave Loboda)

John failed to pick up on Paul's cricket reference, offering instead one of his mock stage announcements: they'd had a request from Martin Luther, he said (either he stuttered in the middle of the name, or the request was from "Martin *and* Luther"). This was much more likely to be a reference to Martin Luther King than to the German Protestant reformer of the 16th century. Writing off that performance of 'Get Back' as a rehearsal, they readied themselves for another shot at the song. John and George went into a gentle rhythmic bounce and tapped their feet, and after a sharp count-in of "One, two, three, four," The Beatles began the song's muscular intro once more. John was playing the song's distinctive lead-guitar part well now, despite the cold. He later told an interviewer that he was allowed the occasional guitar solo when Paul was "feeling kind" or guilty for getting so many songs on the A-sides of The Beatles' singles.

Soon after the music got underway on the rooftop, Apple's front door was locked. The staff expected the noise to attract some attention, but they didn't want to deal with any curious intruders for a good while yet, not until The Beatles had had a chance to play and record a decent quota of songs.

There was much craning of necks as people gathered in Savile Row, but while their playing was coming over loud and clear, The Beatles themselves weren't visible from the street. Unwittingly, they had succeeded in turning Beatlemania on its head. Back in their touring heyday, they could be seen on stage, but the shrill screams of teenage girls often made it impossible to hear their music properly. Today, for the people down in the street, the opposite was true: they could be heard but not seen.

The Beatles *were* visible to the lucky people who worked on the upper floors of adjoining buildings, who could open their windows and enjoy the performance from the comfort of their offices. Then there were the intrepid people who ventured out on the roofs of Mayfair to obtain a better vantage point. One of these was an 18-year-old trainee chartered accountant called Sidney Ruback, who was working for a company called Auerbach Hope in the part of Regent Street directly behind Savile Row. "I was having sandwiches with my work colleagues in the office, which I think was on the third storey of the building. Suddenly we heard this cacophony, and we went to the window and we could see people playing musical instruments on the roof, but from that distance we couldn't make out who they were."

A plan was hatched among a few young Auerbach Hope employees to get closer to the action. "I'm quite reserved, so it was probably one of the others who suggested it. But we climbed out of the window onto our roof, and we scampered over the roof and went up a fire escape to the roof opposite, which was Savile Row. We used a drainpipe as well; in *Let It Be* you can see a few of us coming down a drainpipe. We walked along and suddenly found ourselves standing about 10 to 15 feet away from The Beatles."

As well as appearing in the film, Sidney has pride of place in a well-known black-and-white photograph of the concert: he can clearly be seen in the left of the picture, standing in his suit and tie next to the large skylight on the neighbouring roof as the band plays. "I can't believe how much hair I had at that time," he laughs.

For the Twickenham and Apple rehearsals, Michael Lindsay-Hogg had used a three-man camera team, but this was now expanded to 11 for the rooftop show. There were several cameras on the roof of No. 3 itself, a few in the street, and another on a roof across the street, shooting at an angle towards the left-hand side of the Apple building. Michael says today that permission was probably obtained to site a camera on this roof, and that he doesn't remember it being a problem: he believes this wasn't one of the tailoring businesses.

Paul Bond, the clapper boy during the Twickenham and Apple sessions, found himself in exactly the right place for the development of his career. "Either Michael Lindsay-Hogg or Tony Richmond said, 'Listen, Bonders has been with us all this time. We can't have him just sitting downstairs loading away.'" They gave him a camera and suggested that while the rest of the camera team focused on The Beatles' performance, he could scuttle about and film people on other roofs, looking out of windows and walking about below.

"So I was all over the place with my own little camera, filming pretty girls climbing over things in miniskirts and boots, and people climbing out of windows and going up ladders. It was a bit wibbly-wobbly, but nevertheless it was wonderful to get that sort of material. Then I was put down in the street to film all the old colonels walking past, saying, 'What's all this noise? What's all this rock-a-boogie going on?' That was very funny." "Bonders" can be spotted in photographs of the event, perching in a camelhair duffel coat behind his camera and shooting at the incidental action away from the main attraction.

As The Beatles finished that spirited version of 'Get Back', John made another mock announcement, saying they'd had a request from "Daisy, Maurice and Tommy", whoever they might have been, and they played a fragment of another new song: 'I Want You (She's So Heavy)', as it was known when it eventually appeared on *Abbey Road*. As they played, a tape recorder picked up a reporter interviewing a young woman in the street below.

"Do you know what you're listening to at the moment here?" he asked.

"No, I don't, really," she replied.

"You don't know?"

"No," she repeated, before venturing a guess: "Is it The Beatles?"

"It's The Beatles, yes." The interviewer continued with some dull questions about whether she bought their records (sometimes), whether she'd like to see them play live again (yes, very much), and who was her favourite Beatle (Ringo, though she liked them all).

Michael suggested they move on from 'Get Back'. George's nifty little guitar riff brought the band into John's 'Don't Let Me Down'. It sounded magnificent up there on the roof, with impassioned vocals from John, harmony vocals from Paul and George, interlocking guitar and bass, and cool piano fills from Billy Preston. But The Beatles were really starting to feel the cold now. The air temperature was a fairly mild 8° or 9°C down in the street, but significantly colder 50 feet above it, and the 11½ mile per hour west-southwesterly wind was blowing right at the front of the building and into their faces, creating considerable wind chill. It would have felt more like 2° or 3°C to The Beatles and the technicians up there.

More than 50 miles south, on the Sussex coast, a very different kind of performance was taking place at an even loftier location. From a distance, it looked as if a succession of old women were being forcibly flung off Beachy Head, Britain's highest chalk sea cliff. The women were being launched by a peculiar machine and were plummeting 500 feet and landing violently on the rocks below, where there was a pile of bodies forming. Concerned policemen rushed to investigate and found a BBC production team filming on location for the forthcoming series *Q5*, featuring the comedian Spike Milligan. Spike had conceived a sketch featuring the finals of the Grandmother-Hurling Championship, and the "bodies" chucked off the cliff were dummies, dressed in old-fashioned grandma-style clothing.

Vincent Lankin was walking down Regent Street in London that lunchtime with his grandmother. It was the day before his eighth birthday, and as a special treat he was skipping school and being taken to the Golden Egg – one of a chain of colourful restaurants serving delicious pancakes and other comfort food on oval plates. Vincent and his grandmother had travelled into town from Stamford Hill in north London, using the recently opened Victoria Line of the Underground. "In those days," says Vincent, "to go to the West End was a big treat, and you dressed accordingly. Everybody else around you was smartly dressed too. I wore a shirt and trousers and a tie, with a jumper and a duffel coat, because it was cold. She was a typical Jewish grandmother – she'd say, 'Do your coat up!'

"As we were making our way on Regent Street, we saw a crowd spilling out of a side street, and then we could hear the music. I could hear the bass before I heard anything else. We walked down Burlington Street into Savile Row, and I remember hearing them sing 'Don't Let Me Down'."

John Lennon fluffed one of the verses to the song, smiling as he forgot the lyrics and sang gibberish instead. But nobody outside The Beatles' circle was any the wiser, because this was the first time they had heard 'Don't Let Me Down', the vocals weren't crystal-clear, and anyway, John had sung plenty of nonsense before about walruses, cornflakes and multicoloured mirrors on hobnail boots. The title of 'Don't Let Me Down' had already appeared as a line in 'Hey Jude' a few months before – an example of the cross-pollination and slightly incestuous lyric-borrowing that occurred within The Beatles' oeuvre, another example being the line "See how they run" in both John's 'I Am The Walrus' and Paul's 'Lady Madonna'. And the opening melody of the chorus to 'Don't Let Me Down', with its high note (A♭) descending one tone (F#) and then another tone (E) before rising back up a tone again (F#), finds an echo in the start of the chorus to 'Give Peace

A Chance', composed by John later that year (though that song is in the key of C).

"We still didn't know who it was up there on the roof," says Vincent. "My grandmother must have asked someone there who it was, and someone said, 'It's The Beatles.' I was surprised because I hadn't heard about The Beatles for a while: I'd thought it was all over for them, or they'd been hibernating or something. More people were drifting towards the music now and it was getting crowded, but it was all very friendly. I used to go to the market in Petticoat Lane, so I wasn't afraid of crowds. I noticed the traffic had come to a standstill, and I remember seeing a nice white E-Type Jaguar in front of me and commenting on it to my grandmother."

Alan Bennett was an 18-year-old apprentice coat-maker working for the distinguished tailoring business of Huntsman, which had been in the street for 50 years and whose shop was eight doors away from The Beatles, at 11 Savile Row. But Alan worked in the fifth-storey tailors' workshop behind the Row, whose address was Heddon Street, off Regent Street. "Our building went from Savile Row right through to Heddon Street. I heard them start up the music, and I could tell it was coming from the Apple building, so I went to see what was happening. I got up on the roof at the Heddon Street end, and went over another couple of roofs. I think I ended up about four or five buildings away from The Beatles." One older Huntsman employee who enjoyed the music was the salesman Brian Lishak, who raced up to the roof of the company's building in Savile Row.

Two doors from Apple in the other direction from Huntsman was the tailoring firm of Hawkes at No. 1 Savile Row, where 22-year-old Malcolm Plewes was working as a cutter on the ground floor. "Most of the cutters were in their fifties, and I was one of the youngest. We heard the commotion, and word soon got round that it was The Beatles. We knew that they had offices there, anyway. I dropped my shears and went up in the lift, and a couple of the other youngsters made their way up too."

From the roof of No. 1, Malcolm had a clear view across the roof of No. 2 – the building occupied by Wain, Shiell & Son – to The Beatles' performance area. "It was such an exciting thing to see: I'd seen John Lennon's psychedelic Rolls-Royce parked in the street sometimes, and I'd see Ringo walking around there, but I'd never seen all The Beatles in person before. I remember seeing a hell of a crowd down below, and people had climbed on the big red postbox on the other side of the road, to see if they could get a better view." Other daring spectators, captured by Paul Bond with his roving camera, were perched precariously among the chimney pots of Savile Row. Never had the roofscape of Mayfair been as thoroughly explored as it was on that extraordinary day.

Although Apple's front door was locked for most of the time, the company hadn't shut up shop for the day, and Debbie the receptionist was still letting in the occasional visitor. "We were still open for business," she says, "so if someone had an appointment to see Derek Taylor or somebody else, they'd come in, or they might come in with an enquiry." One friend of The Beatles who was admitted that day was the actor Terence Stamp, who lived in one of the Albany apartments nearby. Having recently split up with the model Jean Shrimpton, Terence was on his way to a new life in India that day; but before travelling to Heathrow Airport he popped in to listen to the music and say hello.

The songwriter David Martin was contracted to Freddy Bienstock's Carlin Music, based at 17 Savile Row, and was on friendly terms with his musical neighbours at Apple. "I came in by train that day and I was on the way to Savile Row, and as I was walking up Vigo Street I heard this amazing sound, which became louder as I approached Savile Row. My first thought was that somebody was playing a Beatles record really loud: I had no idea they were playing live.

"Curiosity led me to walk up the steps into No. 3, and I went in, but the music was very loud and the receptionist and I couldn't hear each other speak, so we used a kind of sign language for a while, pointing upstairs. I got in the lift and walked up to the roof, and I crept as unobtrusively as I could and sat down on a wall where there were already about a dozen people sitting, underneath one of the cameras. I think a lot of them were Apple staff. The Beatles were making the most wonderful sound, but it was very relaxed and easy-going: between songs they'd have a chat and make some jokes, and people would talk about the positions of the cameras, and they'd talk about the song they were going to play next. They weren't under the pressure they would have been under if they were playing a proper concert to thousands of people."

After 'Don't Let Me Down' The Beatles tackled 'I've Got A Feeling'. Like 'Get Back', this is a simple but effective song in the key of A, enhanced by some nice chord variations and guitar riffs. Lyrically, the McCartney section of the song had been inspired by his relationship with Linda Eastman. The location of Paul and Linda's first encounter – the Bag O'Nails in Kingly Street – was just a matter of yards behind The Beatles as they played the song. Georgie Fame & The Blue Flames had been playing in the club that night.

Linda wasn't on the roof to watch the concert that day, perhaps preferring a quiet and restful day at Cavendish Avenue as she was about two months pregnant with the first child she would have with Paul. Their daughter Mary would be born seven months later. Also, she had her six-year-old daughter, Heather, to look after.

After they finished 'I've Got A Feeling', John threw in one of his musical teases, singing "Ooh! My Soul" – the title of a Little Richard song that The Beatles used to play. Paul's screams in 'I've

Got A Feeling' perhaps reminded John of Paul's talent for impersonating the rock'n'roller's raucous vocals.

John also made a couple of quips, including "Can you hear me, mother?" This was a popular catchphrase flogged to death by the northern comedian Sandy Powell that John would have heard as a boy on radio and television. What he probably didn't know was that it was Powell's birthday that day: born just after the beginning of the century, the comedian had just turned 69.

Their hands were feeling the cold badly now, and Ken Mansfield had the perfect solution for warming George's fretting hand: he lit several cigarettes at once and held the orange burning ends near the guitarist's fingertips. Michael suggested that The Beatles pop their heads over the edge of the roof, thus confirming their identity to their gathering audience, but − perhaps wisely − they decided not to, and cracked on with 'One After 909'. This was a rollicking blast from The Beatles' past that the public had never heard before, and the band played it with gusto.

As the number ended, John sang a variation on a line from 'Danny Boy' that Beatles scholars still argue about: "Oh Danny boy", followed by either "the Odes of Pan are calling" or "the Isles of Ken are calling" or something similar.

Dating from the late fifties, 'One After 909' is a very early product of John Lennon's lifelong obsession with the number nine, which would later result in titles such as 'Revolution 9', the sound collage on the White Album, and '#9 Dream', first released on his 1974 album *Walls And Bridges*. He had noticed the recurrence of nines in his life, and considered it his lucky number. He was born on the ninth day of October (and once stated incorrectly in an interview that October is the ninth month of the year), and after he was born he lived briefly at 9 Newcastle Road, Liverpool − the home of his mother, Julia. At the age of 11 he painted a picture of men playing football, with the number nine appearing prominently on the shirt of the player in the foreground (the picture later became part of the artwork of his *Walls And Bridges* album). Brian Epstein first saw The Beatles play at the Cavern on November 9, 1961, and The Beatles signed their first EMI recording contract on May 9, 1962. After The Beatles' break-up, John would become absorbed in a book on numerology that explained how to convert names into numbers via the Hebrew alphabet, and learned that "John" has a mystic value of nine, as do "Paul" and "Ringo".

Tipped off in Fleet Street that something unusual was happening in Savile Row, the *Daily Express* dispatched a reporter and a photographer – Tom Brown and Mike Stroud, respectively – to find out exactly what. They hailed a taxi, but the journey became frustratingly slow and, finding themselves in motionless traffic in Regent Street, they hopped out of the cab and ran as fast as possible towards the noise they heard. Tom had caught the news last year that The Beatles had spent half a million on a building here, so he had his suspicions. They arrived at the south end of Savile Row to see throngs of people staring up at the roof of No. 3 as the music continued. Tom knocked on Apple's front door, but when they were refused admittance they decided to gain access to one of the buildings on the opposite side of the road, where they asked permission, went up in a lift and emerged on another roof, which gave them a fine view.

Tom later described the experience: "We knew right away who it was – it couldn't have been anyone else. The whole place was littered with cables, microphones and amps. There were sound engineers, hangers-on and quite a few girls, including The Beatles' wives and girlfriends. There was not much musical appreciation, because the sound was just being carried away on the wind. The other thing, of course, is we now know that those were new songs that no one had heard before. So they were in no way recognisable. But you could certainly tell it was The Beatles. I think the surprising thing was seeing all four of them there at all. There had been numerous reports in the papers of bust-ups and suggestions that they had already split up. So it was a big thing to actually see them all together and performing…"

Tom Brown wondered about the legality of what The Beatles were doing: the police did not seem to be intervening, but surely they couldn't get away with creating such a major disturbance in the middle of London. So he and Mike came down from the roof and walked towards West End Central to make some enquiries. "We went round to the police station and we just asked the obvious question – were they going to stop it? The guy behind the desk said no, they were happy for The Beatles to have their fun. Apart from the fact that it had brought that part of London to a standstill, it wasn't doing any harm. At least that's the way he saw it. It was something different, in the spirit of the time. So at that point they were happy to let them play."

In the days leading up to the performance, Chris O'Dell had had a fantastic vision of the impending event. She imagined that The Beatles would blast their music out across the whole of London. The sound would flood out into the West End and then spread north, south, east and west, reaching the ears of thousands upon thousands of people. In reality, the music could be heard clearly within a localised area, quickly losing its clarity and volume beyond that. Word had spread around parts of Mayfair and Soho that it was The Beatles making all the racket, but by no means did everybody receive that message: there were countless people passing by in the vicinity who heard the noise and were mystified by it, only learning hours later what it was all about. A prime example is Andy Taylor, who was 17 years old and working in the postroom of an advertising agency in Holborn, east London. "There was another man who worked there as a messenger, called Eddie; he was a lovely little man, and I don't want to be unkind, but he was a bit simple-minded and lived in a bit of a fantasy world. He'd come in and say things like 'I've just seen a tiger in Oxford Street!' And people would say, 'Oh... all right,' to humour him. On that day in January 1969, he came back from delivering something and said, 'The Beatles are on the roof!' And of course, we all thought he meant there was an infestation of beetles, and we thought he was talking about *our* roof. Anyway, about 15 minutes later I had to deliver some artwork to somewhere in Glasshouse Street, by Piccadilly Circus, so I took a cab, and as I got nearer to my destination I realised I could hear something. I could hear it was music, and it was quite loud, but it was a very muddy sound, and it didn't click with what Eddie had said about The Beatles on the roof.

"We accept it now because we know it happened, but you have to remember that back then, nobody would ever dream that The Beatles would suddenly be playing on the roof of a building in London – it was such a weird concept. It was unheard of then for a rock band to be playing in the street in London in the middle of the day. So I delivered the artwork and went back to the agency, and it was only much later, when I saw the news, that I realised what I'd missed. If only I'd known it was The Beatles, I'm pretty sure I could have walked to Savile Row and gone into one of the buildings nearby and said, 'I've come to deliver some artwork,' and gone up on the roof and watched the show."

There was two-way traffic in Savile Row back then, and now it was at a standstill in both directions. It was only necessary for a single vehicle to stop, as the driver and passengers rubbernecked out the window to take in what was happening, for a serious tailback to be created. And tailbacks led to tailbacks: the blocking of Savile Row and other smaller streets began to cause problems in the major thoroughfares, such as Regent Street, which in turn affected Oxford Street. Ford Escorts and Vauxhall Victors were nose-to-tail with Minis and Singer Gazelles, and many of them were tooting their horns as motorcycles and bicycles tried to weave around them. The Beatles had attracted crowds and brought the traffic to a halt in this part of London before – especially around the London Pavilion, at Piccadilly Circus, which had hosted the world premieres of their films, *A Hard Day's Night* in 1964, *Help!* the following year and *Yellow Submarine* in 1968, with the group in attendance and besieged by fans each time.

On that clamorous Thursday, as a chorus of car horns mingled with the music, there was some timely advice in the latest edition of *Practical Householder*, available for two shillings from newsagents' shelves across London, on "Dealing with Noise from Next Door". The magazine lamented that "Undoubtedly some people enjoy making a noise and so make more noise than their neighbours like," explained that noise "can travel not only in air, but in and through solid material, such as wood, bricks, and metal", and recommended that "if you have a noisy neighbour and if all attempts to reach a friendly arrangement fail, you can consider taking legal action".

The smiles on their faces showed that The Beatles were certainly enjoying the act of making a noise that day, and their music was certainly penetrating through many hard surfaces, including walls, ceilings and doors. But their next-door neighbour skipped the part about "a friendly arrangement" and went straight for the legal action. Stanley Davis, who worked at the wool merchants Wain, Shiell & Son at 2 Savile Row, called West End Central to complain about the noise. "It's disgraceful. I want this bloody noise stopped!" he fumed, saying it had seriously inconvenienced his switchboard operators, who couldn't hear anyone properly.

He was just one of a series of grousers, which included someone at the Royal Bank of Scotland across the road – ironic, given that this was the same institution on whose roof Vicki Wickham, Cathy McGowan and Rosemary Simon were enjoying the concert.

The mounting complaints, together with the worsening traffic chaos, caused the police in Savile Row to drop the laissez-faire attitude that Tom Brown had noticed, and the station sergeants there began sending out orders. One of the police constables attached to the station was 25-year-old Ray Shayler, who was just about to go out on patrol. "We could hear the noise from the other end of Savile Row. Another officer was assigned to the incident, whose beat included Savile Row, but he had only just joined – it was his first month. I had the adjacent beat and I had nearly three years' service, so I said to him, 'Do you want me to go as well?' and he said yes."

"I could hear the music clearly as I went down the road," says Ray. "My wife was a bit of a Beatles fan at the time, so I recognised the sort of music it was. There was quite a crowd in the street by this time." Ray approached Apple's big white front door, where he became the vanguard of a multi-pronged police operation, conducted from West End Central, to shut down the noise and ease the congestion in Savile Row.

When the police began knocking at the door, the receptionist Debbie Wellum alerted Jimmy Clark, the company's doorman. "Jimmy was actually more than a doorman: he was meant to be my minder, because of the weird people we had coming in to Apple. There had been a couple of occasions when things got a bit hairy and he had to escort people out of the building. I had a special number to phone him on, and if I called it he knew he'd have to come down. So Jimmy came down and he opened the door, told the police to go away, then closed the door and locked it again. But the police carried on beating on the door."

In the meantime, The Beatles were still playing. After they brought 'One After 909' to an end, there was a discussion between the basement and the roof about which song they should play next, and they settled on 'Dig A Pony', but John was uncertain of the lyrics. Having already fluffed a line in 'Don't Let Me Down', he didn't want to let everyone down again. He remembered that he had some lyrics scribbled down on paper in the studio, so he asked Mal Evans to fetch them. When the words arrived on a clipboard, that didn't entirely solve the problem: John wouldn't be able to read them as he played unless they were propped on a music stand, or something similar. "I'm not too sure if there was a music stand in the basement, but anyway it would have taken five minutes to go all the way down to get it," says Kevin Harrington. Kevin offered to hold the lyrics up for John, but couldn't find a good place to stand. "If I'd stood there to John's right I would've been in the way of Ringo, and if I'd stood to John's left I would've been in the way of George. So I decided to get down on my knees in front of John with the lyrics. That worked, though I think my knees were hurting a bit by the end."

John, Paul and George started to play the opening riff of the number, but Ringo was holding a cigarette and called "Hold it!" Once he was ready, they started the song again. After the lumbering riff, the song settled into a breezy 3/4 time, which was a time signature that came very naturally to John Lennon, who had used it previously in songs including 'You've Got To Hide Your Love Away' and 'Norwegian Wood', and would employ it again later on 'Happy Xmas (War Is Over)'. John later said of the cryptic lyrics: "I was just having fun with words. It was literally a nonsense song. You just take words and you stick them together, and you see if they have any meaning. Some of them do and some of them don't." He may not have counted the number of notes he sang unaccompanied at the beginning of each verse of the song: his favourite number, nine.

Shortly after John sang the "road hog" line, and as he sang the word "penetrate", there was some entertaining body language from George, who descended briefly to the roof onto his left knee in front of him while still playing his guitar. This looked like a humorous gesture, as if he were either mocking Kevin's pseudo-reverential act of kneeling, or sending up the classic rock custom of trading a riff with another guitarist, or both. John responded by lifting his guitar neck and leaning back to strike another parodic rock-star pose. Just over a minute later, after a whoop from Paul and a high "ohhh" from John, George played one of his gorgeous, fluid solos, the notes gliding over John's minor and flattened-seventh chords.

"It was fabulous to see them playing and giggling amongst themselves," says Vicki Wickham. "The Beatles were in great spirits. All the animosity between them, which we all knew about, seemed to have gone. And we were laughing about John's fur coat, which looked too small for him."

"Thanks, brothers," said John after the number ended, adding that his hands were so cold that he was having difficulty playing the guitar chords. There was a pause as Alan Parsons changed recording tapes, which The Beatles and Billy Preston idly filled with an unremarkable instrumental version of 'God Save The Queen' in the key of G, as if to acknowledge the presence in the building of Her Majesty's police, though it was unlikely that they were aware of them yet.

There was a police post by the Underground station at Piccadilly Circus: a tall, narrow box with a light on top, smaller than a police box, with a telephone inside. PC Ken Wharfe, still on traffic duty, saw the light on the post flashing and answered the call. "I picked up the phone and recognised the sergeant's voice, and he asked me if I could hear all the noise. I couldn't − all I could hear was traffic – but he asked me to get my colleague at Shaftesbury Avenue and go and sort it out."

Ken and his colleague walked up Regent Street. "There was this wave of girls coming out of various streets, running towards Savile Row. I soon realised what it was, because it was just a fantastic sound, ricocheting around the buildings. It was unmistakably the sound of The Beatles, and we knew that The Beatles were based in Savile Row, but I didn't imagine at that point that they'd be playing on the roof. By the time we got round there, there were quite a few people in the street, and there was almost a party atmosphere."

"Jimmy was still trying to keep the police at bay," says Debbie. "But they kept knocking, and through the window I saw this Black Maria driving past, and that worried me a bit. Eventually we had to let the police in." Black Marias – the popular term for police vans – were vehicles that were often used to transport prisoners to jail or to court. They could also be used to take people into custody after a multiple arrest, which is why the van's appearance made some people worry that The Beatles were about to be arrested and hauled off to jail.

George Martin was in the building, though he had no official capacity that day, with Glyn Johns in charge of the recording in the basement. Martin, whose traditional upbringing compelled him to respect British men in uniform, became seriously concerned when the officers intervened. "This policeman said if we didn't let them in, they were going to arrest everyone in the building," recalls Dave Harries. "George Martin went as white as a sheet, which I thought was hilarious."

Ray Shayler explains that the purpose of the Black Maria was to transport more police officers to the scene. "It sounds terrible, 'Black Maria', but it wasn't there in case we lifted The Beatles. It had brought officers there because we suddenly had a lot of people and traffic to control. They were just trying to keep the roads open, and also to divide the crowds to make sure there wasn't a crush and there were no people fainting."

"The street was blocked: people were shoulder to shoulder," says Vincent Lankin, who remembers seeing the Black Maria pull up. "Four or five policemen got out of that and started taking control of the traffic."

"The taxi drivers weren't happy – they were shouting and hollering," says Paula Marshall. "The rest of us were having a great time, just listening to the music." Paula was standing by the steps leading to Apple's basement studio when she and her friends were asked to "move on" by the police in charge of crowd control. "We just walked across the road, away from it a bit, and stood there. They kept asking us to move on, and we walked round the block and came back."

"It was like a parade," says Leslie Samuels, "with all these people lined up on the sidewalks on both sides of the street. Except that it wasn't a parade – they were trying to have normal Savile Row traffic. Probably, if I hadn't had the dog with me, I would have gone climbing up buildings. But Brian weighed 50lb and I didn't think he'd do well on steps or stairs: he'd never used those before, and I didn't want him to freak out."

Paula Marshall also decided not to do any climbing that day, but for a different reason: "I was wearing a miniskirt, so I don't think it would have been a good idea."

Back at the front door, Debbie and Jimmy had relented and allowed the first officers to enter. "The police came in," says Debbie, "and they were filmed as they came in. They didn't look happy: they looked angry and displeased at what was going on, and I felt a bit threatened and very nervous." Nevertheless, she managed to stall them to allow The Beatles' performance to continue for a while, saying that Mal Evans would come down to talk to them. There was a further delay as Jimmy went up to the roof to fetch Mal. "Mal decided not to take the lift down, but to walk down the stairs, taking his time," says Debbie, "and about 10 minutes later he talked to the police. They were saying, 'You can't do this,' and 'It's too noisy, we're getting complaints, and charges will be pressed.'" Mal tried to placate the policemen, explaining that The Beatles were just making a recording, and that it would be finished fairly soon. But the officers had their orders, and were keen to get to the scene of the crime – the roof itself – as quickly as possible.

"I remember Mal telling them they couldn't all go up, because the roof was unstable and there were already people up there. Otherwise, we were thinking that if they all went up there, they might have arrested a Beatle each! But Mal took one of them upstairs."

"We all thought we would probably be arrested up on the roof, but so be it," says Michael Lindsay-Hogg. "I was more nervous than The Beatles were, because I was an American and I thought I'd be deported or something."

Alan Parsons later claimed that the frisson of danger represented by the police spurred The Beatles on as they performed. The "slight naughtiness" of playing up here on the roof in Mayfair, he said, "making a lot of noise and disturbing the neighbourhood and local offices and stuff, I think that gave them the necessary adrenaline rush to really enjoy it".

Some of the citizens walking in and around Savile Row, wondering what all the noise was about, were smoking pipes. It wasn't unusual back then for men to puff away at a pipe full of tobacco as an alternative to smoking a cigarette or cigar. The prime minister of the day, Harold Wilson, was often seen clutching a pipe – which he was allowed to smoke even during his audiences with the Queen – and several male celebrities were known for using them. Every January the Briar Pipe Trade Association hosted a lunch at the Savoy Hotel in the Strand, where it would present the Pipeman of the Year award (later renamed Pipe Smoker of the Year award) to a notable puffer in the public eye. The latest award had just been presented to the actor Peter Cushing, who had pretended to smoke a pipe while playing Sherlock Holmes in a BBC television adaptation of the Arthur Conan Doyle stories. In real life, Cushing himself avoided the habit.

Although it was quite obvious that the previous take of 'I've Got A Feeling' had been a success, The Beatles were having another crack at the song. John might not have noticed that George's rapid, ascending chorus riff had nine notes in it. Towards the end of the song, John slipped in a Bob Dylan line, which he repeated: "Everybody must get stoned", the chorus from 'Rainy Day Women #12 & 35', the song that opened Dylan's *Blonde On Blonde* album from two-and-a-half years before. Standing beside her well-behaved dog in the street below, the American student Leslie Samuels noticed and recognised the line, which may have been a payback for Dylan's '4th Time Around' on the same album. Many people, John Lennon included, suspected this song was Bob's mocking response to the Dylan-influenced 'Norwegian Wood (This Bird Has Flown)' on *Rubber Soul*.

Getting stoned might not have been the best course of action for people in the Apple building at that point. One apocryphal story claims that there was a mass flushing of lavatories as staffers anticipating the arrival of the police disposed of their stashes of illicit substances. But the officers who attended 3 Savile Row were regular beat officers: they weren't Nobby Pilcher's stormtroopers, looking for more rock'n'roll scalps in their war on dope. As Chris O'Dell puts it, "They were the bobbies: they weren't the narcs that had been busting everybody."

Ray Shayler confirms that he and his fellow officers weren't looking for drugs. "We'd gone there as a public-order issue, because there'd been complaints about the noise."

After 'I've Got A Feeling' reached its climax, John threw in yet another of his musical quotations, this time from 'A Pretty Girl Is Like A Melody'. He had referenced the same song nearly a month before, on their second day of rehearsals at Twickenham. Although John and Paul had famously bonded in the early days over their shared passion for rock'n'roll, they were also *au fait* with old-fashioned standards such as this 1919 Irving Berlin tune. Paul has talked about his memory of discussing the 1930 Walter Donaldson song 'Little White Lies' with John soon after they met: "That kind of twenties and thirties song was the platform we took off from."

The Beatles played a little bit of 'Get Back' again before deciding to have another full run-through of 'Don't Let Me Down'. This was a slightly more ragged performance than their earlier attempt, and this time John omitted part of the first line in the first verse. But there was potentially a new interpretation of the chorus now, with John asking not to be taken down from the roof by the gathering police. The first rooftop version, complete with John's entertaining gobbledegook line, was ultimately chosen for the *Let It Be* movie.

Down in the street, the aspiring journalist Leslie Samuels had been scribbling some lines from the songs she had heard in a small notebook. "I still have a tiny, faded, shrivelled-up piece of paper from it," she says, "and I think I can read 'I've Got A Feeling', then 'Dig Pony', and then 'Don't Let Me Down'."

Barbara Bennett returned to Savile Row after her lunch with Laurie McCaffrey at Billy's Baked Potato. "We came back and there was all this kerfuffle in the street, and we couldn't get through the crowds. It was a bowler-hatted time, and there were lots of really 'straight' men who were very angry about the sound from the roof. The Savile Row mob didn't like The Beatles being in the street in the first place: it was their little domain."

Barbara and Laurie stood on the pavement for a few minutes, enjoying the music, until they were able to find a path back to Apple's front door. "And when I got back in, I said to Peter Brown, 'Can I go up on the roof?' And Peter said no, I couldn't do that, and that I had to sort the police out. The police were going berserk, saying they'd had so many complaints. So I said to them, 'Would you like to go on the roof and have a look, and enjoy it?' So they did, and they were quite affable."

Mal's earlier advice that only one policeman should ascend to the roof had been forgotten now. Chris O'Dell, still ensconced by the chimney, watched as a number of policemen were escorted onto the roof by Jimmy, the doorman. One of them, she later learned, had commented on the noise nuisance with one of the most ridiculous lines of the day: "Do you know that this is louder than a transistor radio?"

When the police ascended the stairs and came on to the roof, Paul Bond was perched on the structure housing the door through which they arrived. "Most of the time I was shooting off the roof, but when the police arrived it became apparent that there was more fun to be had. I was directly above them as they came out, and I got an overhead shot of their helmets. They looked quite embarrassed to be there."

Peter Brown eventually became directly involved in the discussions with the constabulary. "The police came up to the roof," he recalls, "and they were telling Mal, 'You're not supposed to be doing this. You can't do this.' He sent them over to me. And they said, 'You can't do this,' and I said, '*Why* can't we do it?' 'Well, you just can't do this.' And I said, 'I don't see why we can't do it,' and they said, 'Well, does your landlord know?' And I said, 'We are our own landlords. We *own* the place. So why can't we do this on the roof of our own property?' And they didn't have any answer to this."

Although they knew The Beatles had been enormously successful throughout most of the sixties, it probably came as a shock to the bobbies on the beat to realise quite how wealthy they were. At a time when many people rented their homes while others bought houses for four-figure sums with a mortgage, the Apple organisation hadn't needed a loan of any kind to snap up this half-a-million-pound Georgian mansion in a prime Mayfair location.

Taking in this information, Ray Shayler and his colleague from West End Central were wondering about the legalities of proceeding with arrests if they had to – if The Beatles and their associates simply ignored the complaints and the presence of the police and continued their performance indefinitely. "We were scratching on the subject," says Ray. "We were thinking that it was a breach of the peace, because while the property may be private, the effect was public. And that's how we worked it out – that's how we were going to deal with it if we needed to. But obviously, it's best to negotiate rather than have to do that. Policing was often a difficult situation and you had to work out how you dealt with it."

There was a consensus among The Beatles, Michael Lindsay-Hogg and Glyn Johns that the group should play one more song, so that they had a little more footage and music in the can for the album and the television special. Ray Shayler remembers that Mal Evans told him and his fellow officers that they had to record one more track, assuring them that the performance would then be finished and the noise would stop. "And so I said, 'If you do that, that's fine. But if you try and play beyond that, then we'll have to take action.' I told him that they might as well be hung for a sheep as a lamb, and play one more number."

Ken Wharfe and his colleague from Piccadilly knocked at the front door and were admitted to the building, where they found several officers already in attendance. "We chatted among ourselves: should we stay or should we go?" says Ken. "But we said that we were never going to see the likes of this again, so we stayed. Had this been an incident involving a burglary or a disturbance, the first guys on the scene would have been the ones to call everybody else off and say, 'We'll deal with this.' But the fact is that nobody was going to call anybody off, because this was a unique occasion. I was 19, and most of the cops were in roughly the same age group, so it would have been very much in their musical psyche to be fans of The Beatles."

The conscientious Debbie Wellum managed to escape briefly from her duties at reception to see The Beatles play. "A girl called Carol Padden, who worked for Derek Taylor, came down to see what was going on. She's a bit nosy like that. She's a lovely lady. And she said, 'Have you been up there yet?' I said no, and she said, 'Well, go up and have a quick look.' She took my place in reception, and I went up but I could hardly get through the door. So I just had a quick peek and stayed for about five minutes, and I went back down again."

Down in Savile Row, the art student Steve Lovering was managing to enjoy the music and have a pleasant conversation as well. "I was chatting to a really nice girl, a Scottish girl who was standing next to me. She was a brunette, and she looked a bit like Sandie Shaw. I suggested we go for a drink later, but she had to catch a train. I never saw her again."

After The Beatles finished their second go at 'Don't Let Me Down', they rounded off the performance with the song they had started it with: 'Get Back'. Despite the deal that had been made with the police, an officer made a remark that caused some confusion and prompted Mal Evans to turn off the Fender Twin amplifiers that John and George were using. Ringo cried "Don't touch that!" and George turned his amplifier back on and Mal revived John's, and they were able to finish the song, with Paul tossing in a spoken section about the song's Loretta character "playing on the roofs again" to the displeasure of her mother, who would have her arrested. As the song ended, there was a final "Yay!" of enthusiasm from Maureen Starkey, eliciting a "Thanks, Mo" from Paul. John lifted the Epiphone Casino off his body, turned to the microphone and inspired peals of knowing laughter for the immortal lines: "I'd like to say thank you on behalf of the group and ourselves, and I hope we passed the audition."

People laughed because the quip was pure John Lennon, and because it was a ridiculous thing for a member of the world's most famous and successful rock group to say. But the significance of the line went deeper. Unbeknown to the public, The Beatles had been especially nervous and anxious before the performance, and some of those heebie-jeebies were caused by genuine fears that they had lost their live mojo after such a long spell away from the stage. One of their possible motivations for playing the rooftop, though it may have been subconscious and wasn't necessarily unanimous, was to satisfy their curiosity about one issue: could they still do it? Could they still cut it? Did they still have that Beatles magic? Or, to put a more positive, McCartneyesque spin on it, they knew they could still do it but they simply wanted to prove to everybody that they could still do it. It was, therefore, a kind of self-audition.

There was an element of irony in the audition quip as well, which even John Lennon might not have realised. It concerned the building on which they had played, and the fact that it had previously belonged to Jack Hylton. The Beatles appear not to have been aware that the impresario had been one of the directors of Decca, a record label with unhappy memories for the band. Seeking a recording contract, they had driven down from

Liverpool to Decca's studios in West Hampstead to audition on the freezing-cold morning of New Year's Day in 1962. They recorded 15 songs, including the early Lennon-McCartney songs 'Hello Little Girl' and 'Love Of The Loved', alongside covers of 'Till There Was You' and 'The Sheik Of Araby'. Notoriously, Decca's A&R men had rejected them, with their manager being told: "Guitar groups are on the way out, Mr Epstein."

The rooftop concert was also a peculiar test for the forces of law and order. Looking back after nearly 50 years, Ken Wharfe believes that the Metropolitan Police behaved admirably in an extremely unusual situation. "I've always thought it was an excellent PR exercise on behalf of the police that we didn't arrest anybody. We saw the event for what it was: a piece of free public entertainment, where nobody got hurt. In a world of growing unrest, as it was, here was a free event for the passing lunchtime Londoners of Mayfair, and people went away with a smile on their faces."

Several of the passers-by that day confirmed that. "Nice to have something that's free in this country at the moment, isn't it?" said one of them, a grinning man in a hat, immortalised in the *Let It Be* film.

"It would have taken a very brave copper indeed with two or three years' police experience to detain The Beatles on the roof of their own property," adds Ken. "In fact, we were effectively trespassing there, because we hadn't been invited, not properly, so it's possible that they could have asked us to leave. Of course, they wouldn't have done that, because it was a really friendly, happy occasion."

The police accompanied the group as they retreated inside the building. "John Lennon and George Harrison wouldn't speak to us, which was fair enough," says Ray Shayler, "and Paul McCartney apologised. Ringo made a joke of it all: 'I'll go quietly – don't use the handcuffs!' or something like that."

Ringo said later that he was disappointed the police hadn't been more aggressive, and that the film would have had a much more dramatic conclusion if he had been physically hauled off his drums and clapped in irons.

Towards the end of the rooftop performance as it appears in *Let It Be*, a senior police officer with a moustache can be seen outside the door of Apple. This was David Kendrick, one of the station sergeants in Savile Row, who despite his earnest and highly authoritative demeanour was only 24 years old then – younger than all The Beatles at the time, even George, who would soon be 26. In 2017, having been retired from the police force for 18 years, David Kendrick told me: "In 1969 I was a Station Police Sergeant attached to West End Central Police Station. This is now 48 years ago and my recollection of the event of the rooftop performance in Savile Row by The Beatles is somewhat sketchy, to say the least. I do recall that I was the Duty Officer at the time of their 'practice' on the roof of premises in Savile Row, and that this caused a total traffic jam in and around the area and the police received many calls to deal with the problem. Acting in my official capacity, I attended the premises with other officers and requested The Beatles to stop playing their music, as it was causing total disruption on the streets below. They did so without any difficulty and the area quickly returned to normality."

After their first "gig" for about two-and-a-half years, it would take a while for The Beatles themselves to return to normality, whatever that meant for them. Still charged with adrenaline from the show and enjoying the warmth of their building again, John, Paul and George chatted excitedly to George Martin and Michael Lindsay-Hogg about how the session had gone. John owned up to missing a line on 'Don't Let Me Down', but that could be edited. George Martin, relieved after the police failed to feel his collar, talked about the performance being a "dry run" for another spectacular event, and enthusiastically conjured the idea of a squadron of helicopters flying over London, blasting out Beatles music from speakers attached to their undersides. George Harrison, trying to make a point as some of the others jabbered away, described another fantasy scenario in which all the rock bands in the world stood on the buildings of London, playing the same music. Here was Chris O'Dell's vision of "The Beatles playing to the whole of London" taken to the nth degree. It sounded for a moment as if they were back in pre-January 10th mode, tossing around ideas for exotic and impossible live shows they might play.

Michael was pleased that they'd filmed "all the cops", but lamented the fact that the group had been invisible to hundreds of people down in the street.

"There won't be more rooftops," said George Harrison.

"No more rooftops," echoed Paul.

George didn't sound too bothered that their repertoire that day hadn't included any of his own compositions. The Beatles had mostly favoured the new songs that had come together well in rehearsal. It was no great surprise that these included 'Get Back' and 'I've Got A Feeling', as these had both been played dozens of times at Twickenham and in the basement of Savile Row. But they had also made at least 40 attempts at George's 'All Things Must Pass' and around 30 attempts at 'I Me Mine' without producing gig-ready arrangements. George had been muttering about eventually making an album of his growing stockpile of songs, so he may have been happy to keep the lid on his tunes for the time being. "It was the Lennon-McCartney axis versus the Harrison axis," says Michael Lindsay-Hogg. "And maybe George thought, 'I don't want to do this, so I'll let them do what they want.'"

As traffic began moving again and a hush gradually descended on Savile Row, people drifted away to resume their lives, and the employees of companies in nearby buildings closed their windows and got back to work. The adventurous people on rooftops made their way carefully back over the tops of buildings, including the trainee chartered accountant Sidney Ruback, who found his way back to the offices of Auerbach Hope in Regent Street, returning through the window he had come out of about 40 minutes earlier. "It wasn't quite as exciting going back as it had been coming."

David Martin came down from the Apple roof and wandered down the road to his office at No. 17. One of the reasons he was going in today was to hear a special recording of a song he had written with his musical partners Jeff Morrow and Chris Arnold. "We'd just had four songs recorded by Elvis, and I was going to hear one of them, 'Let's Be Friends'. That ended up becoming the title track of one of his albums. So I had a double treat that day: seeing The Beatles on the roof, and hearing Elvis sing one of our songs."

"I stayed in Savile Row until all the crowds dispersed," says Leslie Samuels, "because I was just enjoying being there, breathing the same air as The Beatles, which is pretty cool. Then I think I took Brian back on a bus, went down Knightsbridge, and we had a run in Hyde Park before going home." Later she would write a letter to *The Beatles Book Monthly*, saying: "You asked for reports of the live Beatles concert from those lucky enough to attend it. As this concert never occurred, no comments are able to be shared.

"But late in January, I happened to be in Savile Row just as the roof-top telly-recording was taking place. I was unable to see the Beatles, but, oh, what I heard was fantastic. (For all the times from '64–'66 when the situation was see, not hear, it was quite a switch!)"

Mal Evans and Kevin Harrington unplugged and disconnected The Beatles' equipment and carried it all back down into the basement, making several trips in the lift and unscrewing the skylight again so that Paul's bass cabinet and Billy's electric piano could be lifted through it.

Steve Lovering took the tube back to his home in Kensington, still shivering with the cold despite his reefer coat. Vicki Wickham, Cathy McGowan and Rosemary Simon came down from the roof of the bank and walked over the road to chat to their friends at Apple.

Malcolm Plewes went down in the lift to the ground floor of Hawkes, picked up his shears and continued his work. Of the older tailors there, he says, "One or two of them thought it was all good fun, but the majority thought it was 'bloody ridiculous'." Alan Bennett ambled back over the rooftops until he reached the top of Huntsman's workshops in Heddon Street*, then returned to the fifth storey to resume his tailoring work. The older tailors, he recalls, "weren't as interested in the music as the youngsters. They didn't like it disrupting trade in the street."

The people who had complained about The Beatles' "noise", like Stanley Davis of Wain, Shiell & Son, returned to work with the smug satisfaction that peace and quiet had returned to their precious domain. Derek Taylor would get his revenge on them, writing: "When The Beatles gave their wonderful rooftop concert and, however briefly, gave West London a shining hour [sic] of absolutely unique excitement, in 1969, it was the stiffnecked shits of Savile Row who called in the law and had the music stopped."

"The Beatles wanted to play their music and put it out there," says Michael Lindsay-Hogg. "And then, of course, there were the stuffy Blue Meanies next door who wanted to close the thing down. 'This is absolutely outrageous!' 'How dare they!' It was very much the sixties: it was the bowler-hatted men versus the long-hairs. It was the vaguely upper class versus the rebellious working-class youth."

---

* A few years later, Heddon Street entered the rock history books in its own right when it became the location for a David Bowie photoshoot for his breakthrough album, *The Rise And Fall Of Ziggy Stardust And The Spiders From Mars.*

Ken Wharfe returned to West End Central and logged himself in a book at the back of the station. "As I was signing in, this sergeant, the man who had made the call at the police post earlier, came and said to me, 'You got that music turned down, then.' I suppose he was in his late forties.

"I said, 'Hey, Sarge, it was amazing. It was The Beatles on the roof down at the Apple building.'

"And he said, 'Let me tell you something, lad. When I came to London, I was dating a girl in Holborn. Every Wednesday afternoon, duties permitting, we used to go and have afternoon tea at the Waldorf Hotel in the Aldwych and listen to music from a *proper* band. Any group of musicians that is forced to play on the roof of their office has got no future.'"

With all the fuss over The Beatles playing live again, people would have been forgiven for not knowing that January 30 was a significant day in other respects. They were reminded when they saw a crowd gathering and laying wreaths by the equestrian statue of Charles I on a traffic island at Charing Cross. It was the anniversary of the king's execution in 1649 during the dark days of the English Civil War, and various historical groups, including the Royal Stuart Society, were honouring his memory. More wreaths were laid and prayers offered at the Banqueting House in Whitchall, where Charles had been beheaded around 2 p.m. on that day 320 years before.

That Thursday in 1969 was also the 21st anniversary of the assassination of Mahatma Gandhi, and people gathered to pray at the spot in New Delhi, near the River Jumna, where the Indian independence leader had been cremated. That evening there was a service at St Paul's Cathedral in London, given by the Archbishop of Canterbury and attended by Lord Mountbatten and the wife of the prime minister, Mary Wilson, to honour the anniversary. Gandhi was praised for his deeply spiritual life, and Mountbatten ended his eulogy with the words: "May his creed of love and non-violence pervade the peoples of this planet." *The Times* reported that "It was a night of colour and music. Indian singers clad in scarlet, purple and green sang – accompanied by a sitar player – before the service and as the congregation dispersed."

Gandhi's death was commemorated again that evening by the inaugural meeting of a new organisation, the London School of Non-Violence, at St Martin-in-the-Fields church in Trafalgar Square. Organised by Satish Kumar, a follower of the Mahatma, the school's purpose was to study the works of thinkers such as Gandhi and Martin Luther King, and "to examine systematically in depth the strategy, technique and potential of non-violence as a political force, and to do this in realistic terms". After its successful opening night, the school would continue to hold lively weekly meetings.

From Trafalgar Square it was a short walk to the Marquee, the rock club based in Wardour Street, and that evening an obscure group called Feathers was appearing on its stage. This was a rather esoteric multimedia trio, two young men and a young woman who combined folk music with tape recordings and mime performances. They comprised John "Hutch" Hutchinson, Hermione Farthingale, and a singer and guitarist who to avoid confusion with Davy Jones of the Monkees had changed his name from David Jones to David Bowie. In the early seventies he would become a superstar, a pioneer of glam rock, and in 1975 top the US charts with a song co-written with John Lennon. Back in 1969, he was about to experience his first brush with fame. A few days after his Marquee gig, he recorded a demo of a song he was particularly proud of, inspired by the latest Apollo missions and given a title punned on the recent film *2001: A Space Odyssey*. 'Space Oddity', which employed the sound of a Stylophone – just like the one John Lennon had been fiddling with during the rehearsals in the Apple basement – would make the UK Top 10 singles chart later that year.

Militant students were on the march again in London that evening. Dozens of policemen attended the scene as hundreds of young protesters marched to the LSE carrying banners and flaming torches, calling for the college to be reopened. One gave a speech to the crowd, sending a message to the education minister who had called them "thugs" and suggested they be "thrown out on their necks". "We have come here to show Mr Edward Short we are not just a minority. We are challenging the very foundations of society. Mr Short is afraid our ideas will spread beyond the students of the LSE. Students are fed up with being kicked around by the Labour government."

The following evening, Billy Preston watched television with his friend George Harrison at Apple. They switched to BBC2, turned the sound up and enjoyed the show that Billy had recorded recently at the Talk Of The Town.

Nobody knew that The Beatles had just made their final public performance. Indeed, there were many people, Apple staffers included, who imagined that they would play live again in the not-too-distant future – on a proper stage, with a paying audience who could see as well as hear them. As George had said, there would be "no more rooftops". If they pulled a similar stunt again, the police would have been down on them like a ton of bricks within minutes. And nobody was really expecting a gig in the Grand Canyon, the Sahara Desert or a Tunisian amphitheatre. But large, conventional venues such as the Royal Albert Hall and the Roundhouse still looked feasible.

Leslie Samuels had ended her letter to *The Beatles Book Monthly*: "If there are any personal reasons why John, Paul, George and Ringo don't want to give a live concert, I, for one, would love to know them. I know many fans are waiting, patiently, for a chance to enjoy the Beatles' efforts à la 1969."

"When they did the concert on the roof, it opened up possibilities," Derek Taylor later explained. "There was talk all through the back end of 1968 about doing ad-hoc concerts, so after they'd done the concert on the roof everything was up in the air again. 'They may perform again,' we said – because it did go well."

As we now know, events conspired to destroy that dream. Allen Klein took over Apple and drove a wedge between Paul and the other Beatles, and the following year brought their official dissolution. Miraculously, they did manage to record an impressive final album, *Abbey Road*, which featured many of the songs they had tinkered with at Twickenham and Apple that trying January, along with some fine additions – among them 'Come Together' and 'Because' from John. The shining gems, though, came from George: his ballad 'Something' and 'Here Comes The Sun', the latter written in Eric Clapton's sunny garden.

When it came to creating a cover for the album, something of the same spirit that had created the rooftop concert was pervading their default recording studio in north London. After plans for a shoot in an exotic location came to nought, they ended up on their own doorstep again, strolling across the zebra crossing outside the building, somehow creating a masterpiece out of apathy and improvisation. It was "Let's do the show right here" all over again. Several million people have since followed in their footsteps on that sacred strip of road, causing taxi drivers to rage and curse as their journey through St John's Wood is delayed over and over again. Many of them use exactly the same earthy language as the cabbies used in Savile Row back in 1969.

If The Beatles' album releases had followed the chronology of their recordings, *Abbey Road* would have been their final album.

But they still had all those *Get Back* recordings in the can, including the rooftop concert, and after various mixes of the songs were rejected, Klein chose the producer Phil Spector to make an album out of them.

The Beatles' TV special never saw the light of day – at least in the form originally intended. The footage from the *Get Back* project was pushed to the back of a cupboard for a while, until Apple beancounters decided that a movie would be a better bet for recouping the expenses of the project. The film *Let It Be* was a much bleaker animal than the TV special would have been, says Michael Lindsay-Hogg. "If it had been allowed to be a television special," he says, "*Let It Be* would not have had the kind of longueurs that inevitably come from musicians who are slightly tired of being in their own company."

Plans to broadcast *The Rolling Stones Rock And Roll Circus* on the BBC were halted by the Stones themselves, who were unhappy with their performance, having played in a state of exhaustion in the wee hours of the morning. It had been their final public performance with Brian Jones, who would be asked to leave the band in June 1969 and would die in July. Cynics claimed that the Stones had scrapped the broadcast because they had been upstaged by The Who. The show was finally released on video in 1996.

Billy Preston was signed to Apple as an artist in his own right, releasing the album *That's The Way God Planned It*, produced by his friend George Harrison. Derek Taylor's sleevenotes declared, somehow without upsetting too many Christians, that Billy "sings and plays like the son of God". Chris O'Dell gave Billy a more permanent place to live in London. "I found him an apartment in a building called the White House. I remember saying at the time that I'd put the first black man in the White House!"

One potentially entertaining project from that period didn't make it out of the blocks: there would be no musical written by

George Harrison and Derek Taylor about everyday life at Apple. If they had finished it, the work would have been a history piece, as the atmosphere at No. 3 changed considerably when Allen Klein arrived and dismissed many of the staff. One day, the receptionist Debbie Wellum reached the end of her tether and walked out of the building for the last time. "It was so unpleasant and people were so unhappy that they were walking out in droves. And one afternoon something awful happened – and I don't even remember what it was – and I thought, 'Well, that's it, I'm off,' and I walked out and I never went back. I went out to the Virgin Islands and spent six months there."

On the whole, The Beatles' memories of the *Get Back* experience were unhappy. John was characteristically acerbic about the early stages of the project, saying: "It was just such a very, very dreadful feeling being there in Twickenham Studios at eight o'clock in the morning with some old geezer pointing a camera up your nose expecting you to make good music with coloured lights flashing on and off in your face all the time."

Nevertheless, it's clear that John, George and Ringo retained a soft spot for the heights of 3 Savile Row. On April 22, 1969, John chose the Apple rooftop as the location for the official ceremony for changing his middle name by deed poll from Winston (his mother had named him after Churchill) to Ono. Also up there on that day was Barbara Bennett of Apple. "I was asked if I'd go up as a witness. So somewhere there's a document with my signature on it, saying he was now John Ono Lennon." However, British law prevented him from ditching the Winston, so he ended up with two middle names.

In 1971, George went up on the same roof with a group of people from the Radha Krishna Temple to publicise the release of a new album of Hindu devotional songs, *Govinda*, that he had produced for them on the Apple label. And after Ringo bought the

Berkshire mansion Tittenhurst Park from John and Yoko in 1973, he had the original spiral staircase from the Apple building – the one that had taken them from the top floor out onto the roof – transported to his new home.

With The Beatles now disintegrated and pursuing solo careers, it fell to other top-flight rock bands to realise their ideas for ambitious foreign concerts that they'd tossed around early in 1969 before settling for the Apple roof. In October 1971, Pink Floyd travelled to the ancient city of Pompeii, where they were filmed playing live in a Roman amphitheatre. There was no audience, unless you include the cameramen, the band's roadies and a few local children, so the event was an unconscious fulfilment of Yoko Ono's "empty seats" concept. There were the inevitable technical problems that attend the actualisation of a grandiose scheme in a foreign land – problems of the kind that The Beatles would have had to overcome. Struggling to muster enough electricity to power their equipment and lights, they eventually solved the problem by running a long cable through the streets from the town hall.

In September 1978 the Grateful Dead flew to Egypt and performed three concerts by the Great Pyramid of Giza. Some of the band's equipment became stuck in the desert sand and had to be towed by camels, and electrical gremlins interfered with the recording of the first show. But they played to a committed and appreciative audience of fans – Deadheads – who had travelled from California to see the shows, and who were joined by local Egyptians. And during the final show they were rewarded with a total lunar eclipse.

By this time serious money was being offered to tempt The Beatles to re-form and play live again. In 1976 the Los Angeles promoter Bill Sargent put up around $50 million for the four of them to play a televised one-off show, which he thought could make $300 million. Paul said he had received a telegram from

Sargent, offering the money, and he had framed it and hung it on his wall. He told an interviewer: "People have said to me, 'Well, you'll have to do it, won't you? You can't go turning down that sort of money.' But to me, there's more to it than that. It's a group that's broken up, for Christ's sake; what do they want us to do? Re-form just for money? I think that's a bit sordid, for what The Beatles were. It's a bit like puppets, isn't it? I'd like to think that The Beatles came back together, if they ever did, because they really wanted to – musically. That's the only reason I'd ever do it. But the thing is that it's more difficult than meets the eye to get four people together to do that, because even for all that money it would kill me to go on stage and not be very good. I'd hate it. I'd hate it even more to be paid vast amounts just to get up there and for people to come along and say we aren't as good as we were. I'd rather leave it that we *were* as good as we were."

But the offers continued. The promoter Sid Bernstein, who had staged The Beatles' earliest American concerts, paid for a major New York press advertisement featuring an open letter to The Beatles, asking them to play one more show. "Let the world smile for one day," he pleaded. "Let us change the headlines from gloom and hopelessness to music and life and a worldwide message of peace. You four are among the very few who are in a position to make the dream of a better world come together in the hearts of millions in just one day." And three years later, the general secretary of the United Nations, Kurt Waldheim, urged them to play a charity concert for South Vietnamese refugees.

"Look," said Ringo, "people have been asking us to do this thing for so long and offering God knows how much, but they don't seem to realise: we didn't *start* doing it for the money, and we ain't going to end it that way."

Good sense and decency should have halted the demands for a Beatles reunion in December 1980, when John Lennon was shot dead outside the Dakota building in New York, but Paul, George and Ringo were still offered $100 million to get back together for three concerts.

Nowadays, in addition to walking across that zebra crossing in St John's Wood, tourists come to Savile Row to see the building where The Beatles surprised the world with their final live session. But they arrive in lower numbers, because when you stand in that street it's impossible even to see where The Beatles stood, let alone stand in their places. It used to be possible to go up on that roof, and I did that on June 22, 1998, by simply asking somebody at the Council of Mortgage Lenders, who were occupying the building at the time. "Fine, no problem," they said, and I stayed up there for about 20 minutes, wandering around in a quasi-religious daze. The views are fantastic.

The following year, The Bootleg Beatles were allowed to go up there and perform a 30th-anniversary tribute concert. It happened to be a Saturday, so it was a good day for attracting crowds of Beatles fans. Steve Lovering went along, three decades after he had witnessed the original event, and as a rooftop VIP he was invited up to the top of the building to watch the band. "I remember going up in the lift with Mark Ellen, the music writer. It's a really small lift, and we were in there with a lady with very large breasts, and we looked at each other and giggled like 12-year-olds."

On the 40th anniversary, a Friday in 2009, The Bootleg Beatles were denied permission to recreate the performance for a second time, with the police and officials of Westminster Council muttering about "health and safety" concerns, a sure sign that they couldn't think of any other grounds to avoid a small amount of extra work. However, honouring the spirit of the original event, two members of the group defied the ban and mounted the roof to play 'One After 909' and 'Get Back' on acoustic guitars. Other rooftop recreations went ahead in the USA that day, as the tribute band Anthology played on the roof of Broward College in Fort Lauderdale, Florida, and The WannaBeatles blasted out the songs on top of Rippy's nightclub in downtown Nashville, Tennessee.

Later that anniversary year, on a Wednesday in July, Paul McCartney himself played a surprise high-rise mini-concert with his band atop the marquee of the Ed Sullivan Theater in New York City, where he was appearing on the *Late Show With David Letterman*. He played 'Get Back' along with two songs from the White Album – 'Helter Skelter' and 'Back In The USSR' – and highlights from his post-Beatles career, including 'Band On The Run' and 'Let Me Roll It', as crowds gathered and screamed behind metal barriers in the street below and people stared out of their Midtown Manhattan offices. This time round, Paul had obtained official permission and the police were as cool as the NYPD can be.

Inspired by the example that The Beatles set, many other groups have taken to playing on a roof over the years. In March 1987 U2 filmed a performance video of their song 'Where The Streets Have No Name' from the roof of a liquor store in downtown Los Angeles, manifestly without permission since the LAPD showed up and stopped the show, albeit not before the Irish quartet had played 'Streets' four times in an eight-song set. Later that same year Echo & The Bunnymen did the same thing atop the HMV Records store in the eastern section of London's Oxford Street, performing 'Twist And Shout' in a clear nod to The Beatles, whose *Sgt. Pepper*-era image adorned the front of the building that day. In 2012 Blur filmed videos for the song 'Under The Westway' and 'The Puritan' from a rooftop in Notting Hill Gate that wasn't quite under the Westway but within shouting distance.

Since 2009, it has become more difficult to gain access to the roof of 3 Savile Row as an individual, let alone take a band up there and plug in. In 2014 the building was opened as a children's clothing shop by the American retailer Abercrombie & Fitch, and when I made a subsequent request to revisit the roof, it was met with a baffling refusal. "Thanks for reaching out," emailed a corporate communications operative. "Unfortunately, this is not something we are able to approve due to various barriers. Thanks for understanding."

The Beatles' rooftop concert has inspired paintings, cartoons and sculptures. One of the most impressive works is a model of the building with a recreation of the concert on top, painstakingly assembled by the Yorkshireman Bob Bartey and his friend Dave Loboda. In 2013, while Dave made a model of the building, Bob spent much of his spare time fashioning the models of John, Paul, George and Ringo with their instruments, though he had never tried modelling before. "I bought some old figures and just remoulded them, and a lot of it is made of junk, really," he says. "The drum kit is made out of wine bottle tops and keyrings and stuff like that." People on YouTube have seen images of the model, and Bob took it to the International Beatleweek Festival one year. "I think at that point I'd just got Yoko and Maureen on it, sat by the chimney stack. But I've got a few other people on there now. I added figures when I received comments from people. Michael Lindsay-Hogg actually saw it and noticed he wasn't on it! And it's still ongoing."

Bob was 14 years old and at school on the day The Beatles played the rooftop, and he has been fascinated with the event ever since. "I still think it was a great gig – one of The Beatles' best performances," he says. He is one of many thousands of fans who wish they had been in Savile Row around lunchtime on January 30, 1969.

For every teenager who has ever been told to "turn that bloody noise down", the rooftop concert stands as a glorious, rebellious event – the bedroom blast writ large. For an infinitesimal moment in human history, the wheels of industry ground to a halt and the power and glory of rock'n'roll burst through the barricades into the dismal grind of everyday life. And the people who were there – the fans, the shoppers, the film-makers and technicians, and even some of the tailors and policemen – will always feel special. "That was one of the greatest and most exciting days of my life," recalled Alan Parsons. "To see The Beatles playing together and getting an instant feedback from the people around them, five cameras on the roof, cameras across the road, in the road, it was just unbelievable."

Peter Brown, The Beatles' business manager, told me he didn't give interviews very often, but that he was intrigued that I was devoting a book to the rooftop performance. "It *was* a rather strange thing that we did, wasn't it?" he said.

It certainly was. Mighty strange, and pretty marvellous as well.

Selected Bibliography

Badman, Keith: *The Beatles Off The Record*, London, Omnibus Press, 2000

Badman, Keith: *The Beatles: The Dream Is Over*, London, Omnibus Press, 2002

The Beatles: *The Beatles Anthology*, San Francisco, Chronicle Books, 2000

Bramwell, Tony & Kingsland, Rosemary: *Magical Mystery Tours: My Life With The Beatles*, London, Robson Books, 2005

Brown, Peter & Gaines, Steven: *The Love You Make: An Insider's Story Of The Beatles*, London, Macmillan, 1983

Cott, Jonathan: *Days That I'll Remember: Spending Time With John Lennon & Yoko Ono*, London, Omnibus Press, 2013

DiLello, Richard: *The Longest Cocktail Party*, Edinburgh, Mojo Books, 2000

Doggett, Peter: *You Never Give Me Your Money: The Battle For The Soul Of The Beatles*, New York, Vintage, 2010

Dowlding, William J: *Beatlesongs*, New York, Fireside, 1989

Flippo, Chet: *McCartney: The Biography*, London, Fontana, 1989

Harrington, Kevin: *Who's The Redhead On The Roof...? My Life With The Beatles*, London Apcor Books, 2016

Johns, Glyn: *Sound Man*, New York, Plume (Penguin USA), 2015

Lennon, Cynthia: *John*, New York, Crown Publishers, 2005

Lewisohn, Mark: *The Complete Beatles Chronicle*, London, Hamlyn, 1995

Lewisohn, Mark: *The Complete Beatles Recording Sessions*, London, Bounty, 2013

Lindsay-Hogg, Michael: *Luck And Circumstance: A Coming Of Age In Hollywood, New York, And Points Beyond*, New York, Alfred A. Knopf, 2011

Mansfield, Ken: *The White Book: The Beatles, The Bands, The Biz: An Insider's Look At An Era*, Nashville, Thomas Nelson, 2007

MacDonald, Ian: *Revolution In The Head: The Beatles' Records And The Sixties*, New York, Vintage, 2008

Matteo, Steve: *Let It Be*, New York, Continuum, 2014

McNab, Ken: *The Beatles In Scotland*, Edinburgh, Polygon, 2012

Miles, Barry: *Paul McCartney: Many Years From Now*, New York, Vintage, 1998

Miles, Barry: *The Beatles: A Diary*, London, Omnibus Press, 1998

Miles, Barry: *In The Sixties*, London, Pimlico, 2003

Norman, Philip: *Paul McCartney: The Biography*, London, W&N, 2016

O'Dell, Chris: *Miss O'Dell: My Hard Days And Long Nights With The Beatles, The Stones, Bob Dylan, Eric Clapton, And The Women They Loved*, New York, Touchstone, 2009

O'Dell, Denis & Neaverson, Bob: *At The Apple's Core: The Beatles From The Inside*, London, Peter Owen Publishers, 2002

Schreuders, Piet, Lewisohn, Mark & Smith, Adam: *The Beatles' London*, Massachusetts, Interlink Books, 2009

Sounes, Howard: *Fab: An Intimate Life Of Paul McCartney*, London, HarperCollins, 2010

Sulphy, Doug & Schweighardt, Ray: *Get Back: The Beatles' Let It Be Disaster*, London, Helter Skelter Publishing, 1998

Taylor, Derek: *As Time Goes By*, London, Sphere Books, 1974

Thomson, Graeme: *George Harrison: Behind The Locked Door*, London, Omnibus Press, 2016

Wenner, Jann: *Lennon Remembers*, London, Penguin, 1981

Winn, John C: *That Magic Feeling: The Beatles' Recorded Legacy, Volume Two*, New York, Random House USA, 2009

Womack, Kenneth: *Long And Winding Roads: The Evolving Artistry Of The Beatles*, New York, Bloomsbury Academic, 2007